Teaching Students to Become Self-Determined Learners

Other books by Yong Zhao

*Catching Up or Leading the Way: American Education in
the Age of Globalization*

ASCD MEMBER BOOK

Many ASCD members received this book as a
member benefit upon its initial release.

Learn more at: **www.ascd.org/memberbooks**

Teaching Students to Become Self-Determined Learners

Michael Wehmeyer
Yong Zhao

Alexandria, Virginia USA

1703 N. Beauregard St. • Alexandria, VA 22311-1714 USA
Phone: 800-933-2723 or 703-578-9600 • Fax: 703-575-5400
Website: www.ascd.org • E-mail: member@ascd.org
Author guidelines: www.ascd.org/write

Ranjit Sidhu, *CEO & Executive Director*; Stefani Roth, *Publisher*; Genny Ostertag, *Director, Content Acquisitions*; Julie Houtz, *Director, Book Editing & Production*; Joy Scott Ressler, *Editor*; Judi Connelly, *Senior Art Director*; Melissa Johnston, *Graphic Designer*; Keith Demmons, *Production Designer*; Kelly Marshall, *Manager, Production Services*; Trinay Blake, *E-Publishing Specialist*.

All web links in this book are correct as of the publication date below but may have become inactive or otherwise modified since that time. If you notice a deactivated or changed link, please e-mail books@ascd.org with the words "Link Update" in the subject line. In your message, please specify the web link, the book title, and the page number on which the link appears.

PAPERBACK ISBN: 978-1-4166-2893-4   ASCD product #119020
PDF E-BOOK ISBN: 978-1-4166-2895-8; see Books in Print for other formats.

Quantity discounts are available: e-mail programteam@ascd.org or call 800-933-2723, ext. 5773, or 703-575-5773. For desk copies, go to www.ascd.org/deskcopy.

Featured Selection
ASCD Member Book No. FY20-6B (Apr. 2020 PS). Member books mail to Premium (P), Select (S), and Institutional Plus (I+) members on this schedule: Jan, PSI+; Feb, P; Apr, PSI+; May, P; Jul, PSI+; Aug, P; Sep, PSI+; Nov, PSI+; Dec, P. For details, see www.ascd.org/membership and www.ascd.org/memberbooks.

Library of Congress Cataloging-in-Publication Data

Names: Wehmeyer, Michael L., author. | Zhao, Yong, 1965- author.
Title: Teaching student to become self-determined learners / by Michael
    Wehmeyer and Yong Zhao.
Description: Alexandria, VA: ASCD, [2020] | Includes bibliographical
    references and index.
Identifiers: LCCN 2019039566 (print) | LCCN 2019039567 (ebook) | ISBN
    9781416628934 (paperback) | ISBN 9781416628958 (pdf)
Subjects: LCSH: Motivation in education. | Student-centered learning. |
    Mastery learning. | Learning, Psychology of. | Self-culture.
Classification: LCC LB1065.W45 2020 (print) | LCC LB1065 (ebook) | DDC
    370.154--dc23
LC record available at https://lccn.loc.gov/2019039566
LC ebook record available at https://lccn.loc.gov/2019039567

28 27 26 25 24 23 22 21 20   1 2 3 4 5 6 7 8 9 10 11 12

Teaching Students to Become Self-Determined Learners

The Missing Actor in Education

"Perhaps children don't need another reform imposed on them. Instead, they need to be the authors of their own education," wrote Williams College psychology professor Susan Engel in an op-ed piece published in *The New York Times* (2011). Engel, a prolific writer on child development and education, reached this conclusion after following the unusual learning journeys of eight high school students at Monument Mountain Regional High School in western Massachusetts. These students designed and ran their own school within a public high school for an entire semester. During the semester, the students followed their own curriculum, without taking other classes. Although they sought advice from English, math, and science teachers, they were primarily responsible for their own learning, monitoring each other's work, and providing feedback to one another. There were no grades, although the students wrote evaluations of each other. They called their program the Independent Project.

The Independent Project was initiated in 2010 by Samuel Levin, then a student at Monument, at the encouragement of his mother. "Why don't you just make your own school?" she responded when Levin complained to her about how unhappy he and his classmates were about their high school experiences, recounts *Time* magazine writer Alexandria Sifferlin (2013).

So he did.

When he was in the ninth grade, Samuel began with a schoolwide garden tended solely by students. The students showed so much commitment to the garden that some got up early on Saturdays to work with the plants. The level of commitment he found in his classmates to nurture something they had created themselves convinced Levin that the students were capable of more—perhaps even managing their own schooling. "I saw the really amazing and powerful things that happened when high school students stepped it up and were excited about something," Levin said of his experience with the garden project (Sifferlin, 2013).

Levin talked with his school guidance counselor, Mike Powell, about his idea to create a school that would be run by students. Powell extended his support and worked with Levin to get the endorsement of the school principal and superintendent. Amid some pushback from faculty and parents, the school's Curriculum Steering Committee and the board approved the proposed program, and the experiment began in 2010.

The Independent Project proved to be a huge success, at least in terms of the experience of the students who were involved. "The results of their experiment have been transformative," observed Engel. Students who were on the verge of dropping out of school became obsessed with learning. Students who struggled in the conventional classroom flourished in their own school. The project worked well for all kinds of students. "Students, regardless of their previous grades, all produced impressive, substantial, and authentic work," wrote Milton Chen, founding executive director of the George Lucas Education Foundation. "They also learned valuable skills of time management and helping classmates with constructive criticism" (2014).

The Independent Project was even more successful as an education experiment in terms of impact and influence. By all accounts, it was a small endeavor: eight students being allowed to manage their own learning for one semester out of their 12 years, or 24 semesters, in their school careers. The idea was fairly simple and straightforward: let the students own their learning.

The project has caught the attention of many. Stories of the project have appeared in major media outlets such as *The New York Times, The Washington Post,* and *Time,* as well as influential education media such as Edutopia, KQED Mindshift, and the website Public School Review. The project was featured in the popular education documentary *Beyond Measure: The Revolution Starts Now* (Abeles, 2015). A short video about the project went viral on YouTube, with more than 200,000 views since it was posted in 2013. The project was the central topic of a book coauthored by Samuel Levin and Susan Engel published in 2016—*A School of Our Own: The Story of the First Student-Run High School and a New Vision for American Education.* The project has also inspired many parents, educators, and students to start their own Independent Project. The school and Levin have received countless e-mails and visits from people interested in emulating the project.

The success of the Independent Project was the result of growing dissatisfaction with conventional education. It seems to be an answer to the many widely recognized problems of education as it is practiced in most of our schools. It also seems to be an indictment of the numerous failed efforts initiated by governments to improve education. It indicates a new direction for educational change.

Dissatisfaction with Conventional Education

There is widespread dissatisfaction with current education practices among students, parents, and the public in almost every country in the world. This dissatisfaction is rooted in a number of widely recognized and documented problems. Chief among them are the persistent education achievement and attainment gaps among students of different backgrounds, the widespread disengagement of students with schooling, and the unpreparedness of children for a world being rapidly shaped by technological advances.

Left Behind: The Achievement Gap

It is no secret that current education does not serve all children equally well. Vast inequalities exist in education today, as demonstrated by the persistent chasm in academic achievement among different groups of children. Children's family backgrounds play a significant role in their educational achievement. In other words, the socioeconomic conditions into which children are born to a large extent determine their educational outcomes.

In the United States, for instance, children of color and from low-income families have, on average, performed worse than Caucasian children and children from high-income families on virtually all indicators of academic success: standardized test scores, high school graduation rates, and college matriculation rates (Bailey & Dynaski, 2011; Darling-Hammond, 2010; Duncan & Murnane, 2011; Ford & Grantham, 2003; Fryer & Levitt, 2004; Hansen, Levesque, Quintero, & Valant, 2018; Plucker, Hardesty, & Burroughs, 2013; Reardon, 2011). Children's academic performance also varies along geographical lines, with children in certain geographical regions doing better than their counterparts in other regions. Similar gaps exist in other educational systems around the world (Byun & Kim, 2010; OECD, 2016; Zhang & Zhao, 2014).

The natural conditions with which children are born also play a significant role in determining their educational outcomes. Children are born with different intellectual capacities, personalities, and desires (Gardner, 1983; John, Robins, & Pervin, 2008; Reiss, 2000; Sternberg, 1988; Zhao, 2018a, 2018b). These natural-born differences lead to different fates in schools and, in turn, outcomes, because certain attributes are favored and others discouraged in the current education system. The favored attributes contribute to educational success and those children with such attributes do well in schools and enjoy better educational outcomes. Children with less-favored attributes do not fit in the current education system and are deemed failures (Clark, 2016; Zhao, 2012, 2018b). The result is the vast academic achievement gap among children—some become straight-A students with excellent test scores and go on to prestigious colleges, and some cannot even achieve the grades or scores to graduate from high school; some move quickly ahead of others and are placed in gifted and talented programs, while some struggle to even keep pace and are identified to receive special or remedial education.

The first kind of achievement gap, the one associated with children's socioeconomic status and race/ethnicity, has received much attention. It has been accepted as a result of social injustice and economic inequality. It also has been recognized as a matter of grave social and economic consequences if left unaddressed. As a result, closing this achievement gap has been on the mind of many governments in recent decades. In fact, the majority of recent reform efforts launched by governments around the world have targeted the achievement gap linked to poverty and race/ethnicity.

The latter gap (the one associated with differences in talents, interests, and personality) has been largely ignored. Worse, it has been accepted as normal and an expected outcome of education. In other words, the gap is intentional because education, as a sorting mechanism, is intended to differentiate individuals and select them for different opportunities and places in a meritocracy (Zhao, 2016b, 2018b). Consequently, apart (perhaps) from students receiving special education services, children who are not served well by conventional education are simply considered underperforming students. The problem, in other words, is seen as the child and not the education system itself. For far too many parents and students, this gap is a source of dissatisfaction and misery (Clark, 2016). There is increasing recognition that these students are victims of current education practices, and there is growing interest in changing pedagogical practices to meet the needs of diverse learners, resulting in the recent growth of differentiated education, personalized learning, and individualized learning.

The Miserable: Disengagement and Emotional Cost

Another source of dissatisfaction is student disengagement. Many students are not actively engaged with learning in schools. In the United States, the 2017 Gallup Student Poll found that less than half of students are engaged, while nearly a quarter of students are actively disengaged, and another 29 percent are moderately disengaged. The numbers are about the same as in the previous year. The same survey found that only 20 percent of students said that they did not miss school at all in the previous year without a good reason or because they were sick, while nearly 30 percent said they missed school a lot or some. In Australia, a study found that about 40 percent of students are unproductive in a given year (Goss & Sonnemann, 2017).

Another sign of disengagement is dropping out of school. Many students choose to leave school before completion. In the United States, for example, more than one million students drop out of school each year without earning a diploma (Washor & Mojkowski, 2014). About six percent of American high school students dropped out in 2016.

In addition to disengagement, many experience negative emotions about school. According to 2015 results of the largest international education survey, the Programme for International Student Assessment (PISA), more than half the world's 15-year-olds reported feeling very anxious about taking tests and a slightly lower percentage of students reported that they get tense about studying. The same study found that more than a quarter of students do not have a sense of belonging at school (OECD, 2017).

Students are also extremely bored in school. They are "bored out of their minds" (Jason, 2017). The Gallup Youth Survey conducted in 2004 asked teens to select the top three words to describe their feelings in school; half of them chose "bored" and 42 percent chose "tired." Only two percent reported having never been bored in school.

The issues of student disengagement, dropout, anxiety, boredom, and general social, psychological, and emotional well-being have been frequently reported and discussed. They have grave consequences for the students themselves as they go through school, and as adults when they leave school. Consequently, they have serious economic and social consequences for society. Thus, not surprisingly, educators, parents, and policymakers have been frustrated with the failure of educational institutions to engage children in productive activities, provide more engaging experiences, and offer an environment that promotes social, psychological, and emotional well-being in all students (Feldman, Smith, & Waxman, 2017; Gleason, 2017; Washor & Mojkowski, 2014).

The Unprepared: The Talent Mismatch

Another major source of dissatisfaction with education today is its failure to prepare children for a world that has been and will continue to be transformed. It is widely recognized that today's schools are not adequately equipping children with the skills and qualities needed for the future, resulting in a talent mismatch. In other words, the skills and knowledge schools expect children to master are not what the future world needs, and what the future world needs is not being taught in schools.

Education is always in a race with technology (Goldin & Katz, 2008). Gradual technological advances accumulate into a revolution and transform civilization. Such transformation often leads societies to reconsider the value of previously prescribed skills and knowledge. Different societies value different skills and knowledge. What is useful and desirable in one society may not be equally useful or desirable in another. Likewise, what is useful and desirable in the past may become obsolete in the future. Thus, throughout history, societies have engaged in exercises to define and redefine human qualities worth cultivating in schools, especially during times of significant change (Broudy, 1982; Goldin & Katz, 2008).

We are in the midst of major societal change. Starting in the 1970s, waves of technological advancement have led to massive societal transformations that ushered in the Third and Fourth Industrial Revolutions (Schwab, 2015), or the Second Machine Age (Brynjolfsson & McAfee, 2014). Unlike the first rounds of industrialization, the Fourth Industrial Revolution features "smart" machines, or artificial intelligence (AI), and AI-based automation, as well as global networks of things (Executive Office of the President, 2016; Schwab, 2015). These "smart" machines have already brought about disruptive changes and will continue to do so in the future.

Some of the knowledge and skills cultivated by traditional education have been increasingly rendered less valuable or even obsolete by "smart" machines (Pink, 2006; Wagner, 2008, 2012; Zhao, 2012). The goals of technological development are to enhance and extend human abilities, to make human beings more effective and more efficient, help human beings perform tasks that would otherwise be impossible, and free people from mundane, harmful, and dangerous tasks. Over the past two centuries, technology has significantly increased human productivity, extended human capabilities, and freed more humans from mundane and dangerous tasks. A collateral effect is the disappearance of traditional production-line jobs and displacement of some human workers. This occurs because machines have been increasingly equipped with the same knowledge, skills, and other human qualities to perform tasks previously performed by human beings. In fact, machines are much superior to human beings for some tasks, and very often machines cost much less, are consistently obedient, and can work longer hours without complaint than human beings. Machines have gradually taken the jobs schools have traditionally prepared human beings to perform, rendering the prescribed qualities less useful and desirable.

Rote memorization, information processing, and repetitive procedure knowledge are among the first to be rendered less useful by recent information and communication technologies. For example, the best *Jeopardy!* and chess players in the world are computers, demonstrating the superiority of machines' capacity for information storage and processing. Traditionally valued low-level cognitive skills are easily replaceable by machines, as are traditionally valued and machinelike qualities such as following instructions and obeying orders without questioning (Brynjolfsson & McAfee, 2014; Common Core State Standards Initiative, 2011; European Communities, 2006; Frankiewicz, 2019; Partnership for 21st Century Skills, 2007; World Economic Forum, 2016). At the same time, the Second Machine Age (Brynjolfsson & McAfee, 2014) has created opportunities for traditionally undervalued talents to become valuable. For example, when jobs that require rote memorization disappear, the number of jobs requiring higher-order thinking such as creativity increases. As a result, as the manufacturing class declines, the creativity class rises (Florida, 2012). When jobs that favor so-called "left-brain" skills such as linear and logical thinking are automated, the "right-brained"-based talents become more useful and desirable (Pink, 2006).

More importantly, increased productivity brings about more leisure time and disposable income, which allows human beings to expand their consumption beyond physical necessities (Zhao, 2012). Whereas underdeveloped countries must focus on basic survival (e.g., food, clean water, shelter, basic medicine), humans in technologically developed economies are able to invest in the psychological, aesthetic, intellectual, and social needs of its populace. Thus, in developed economies, education, entertainment, health care, travel, fashion, beauty, and other industries that serve psychological, intellectual, aesthetic, and social needs have become as large as (if not larger than) industries that meet the basic needs for physical survival, such as food and housing.

These new industries provide unlimited potential for traditionally undervalued talents to become useful and desirable. For example, interpersonal and intrapersonal talents became very valuable as the counseling industry expanded; all sorts of therapy, personal coaching, and interpersonal communication skills became highly valuable. Artistic talents have become more valuable as more people consume arts in various forms, including visual arts, video games, aesthetically appealing devices and furniture, artisan food, and films. Similarly, the ever-expanding television and video industry has created opportunities for individuals talented in storytelling, acting, and being funny. In other words, some traditionally useless talents have become useful (Zhao, 2018c).

Under the big umbrella of 21st century skills (Partnership for 21st Century Skills, 2007; Trilling & Fadel, 2009) are a host of skills and characteristics that have not been considered important before: communication, critical thinking, creativity, and collaboration (Common Core State Standards Initiative, 2011; European Communities, 2006; Trilling & Fadel, 2009). There are numerous other skills, abilities, and characteristics proposed to be valuable in the new age that have not been valued in traditional education: dispositions (Costa & Kallick, 2013), creativity and innovation (Florida, 2012; Wagner, 2008, 2012), right-brained skills (Pink, 2006), entrepreneurial skills and mindset (Wilson, Vyakarnam, Volkmann, Mariotti, & Rabuzzi, 2009; World Economic Forum Global Education Initiative, 2011; Zhao, 2012), personal qualities (Duckworth & Yeager, 2015), global competencies (Reimers, 2009; Zhao, 2009a, 2009b), mindset (Dweck, 2008; Gardner, 2007), and noncognitive or soft skills (Brunello & Schlotter, 2010; Levin, 2012; World Economic Forum, 2016).

Schools, by and large, have not responded to the changes. The majority of schools in the world have continued to insist on teaching the obsolete skills, while ignoring the ones that have become essential in the new world. The result is the inevitable talent mismatch, which has already negatively affected the world economy and the lives of millions of people who fail to find meaningful work (Zhao, 2015b). The Hays Global Skills Index (2015), developed by the global recruiting firm Hays in partnership with Oxford Economics, points out:

> Yet, as [labor market] participation rates fell and long-term unemployment increased, businesses have still found it difficult to fill job vacancies. This apparent contradiction—unfilled jobs and high unemployment—is a clear indicator of a mismatch between the skills employers are looking for and the skills possessed by job seekers. (p.11)

The situation of talent mismatch will continue and worsen if education remains the same. Without transformative changes, our children will be woefully unprepared to succeed in the Second Machine Age. They will not be able to enjoy the prosperity promised by the technological advances leading to the Fourth Industrial Revolution.

Failed Reforms

To be fair, there has not been a lack of efforts to address these dissatisfactions. Apart from the bottom-up efforts of educators, education researchers, and businesses to introduce small-scale changes, governments around the world have launched massive top-down reforms to improve education (Schleicher, 2018; Zhao, 2015a; Zhao & Gearin, 2018). Because governments are the most influential actors in education, as they control policies and investment, reform efforts launched by governments have been the primary force shaping the directions of change in education.

Broadly speaking, education reforms launched by governments in the world in recent years have followed two different trajectories. One is to introduce more standardization, centralization, and test-driven accountability into schools, and the other is to allow more local control, reduced testing, and decreased academic burden. Representative of the first trajectory is the United States, Australia, and England. These education systems have made serious attempts to develop nationally centralized curriculum standards, impose national standardized tests to hold schools and teachers accountable, increase competition among schools and students, and favor direct instruction (Zhao, 2012). The No Child Left Behind Act (No Child Left Behind Act of 2001, 2002) and the Common Core State Standards Initiative (2011) in the United States epitomize this trajectory.

Reform efforts in East Asian education systems such as China, Singapore, Hong Kong, and South Korea exemplify the latter trajectory. These systems have been working hard to relax central control of the curriculum, broaden the curriculum beyond core subjects, limit the importance and frequency of standardized testing, and grant more local autonomy. Additionally, these systems have also introduced measures to reduce academic burden, shorten school days, curb tutoring outside school, reduce competition among schools and students, and introduce more child-friendly pedagogies (Zhao, 2014, 2015a).

The two trajectories are in opposition to each other, but they are both rooted in past experiences (Zhao, 2009a, 2018d). The standardization, centralization, and testing trajectory has been the traditional practice in East Asia, while the more local autonomy, broader curriculum, and less testing trajectory has been a feature of Western education. From this perspective, the global education reforms are, in essence, a trade of past strategies and tactics. The reason for this mutual borrowing lies in the different perceptions of problems each education system faces. The most acute education problem perceived by Western education systems is low academic performance and the wide achievement gap, measured by test scores, especially compared to East Asian education systems. This perception is partially a result of international assessment programs, such as PISA and Trends in International Mathematics and Science Study (TIMSS), which have consistently placed East Asian students far ahead of students in the United States, England, and Australia. Traditional practices of East Asian education are thus believed to lead to better academic outcomes and smaller achievement gaps and are worth emulating (Tucker, 2011).

East Asian education systems have been troubled by their students' high anxiety, lack of creativity, low confidence, and poor social, psychological, physical, and emotional health. They believe that education in the West, in particular the United States, holds the solution. Thus they have been drawing inspiration from traditional practices in the West in their attempt to improve education (Zhao, 2009a, 2018d).

The results of the reforms have generally been disappointing. They have done little to make education better. The problems that caused the widespread dissatisfaction remain. The reforms have not improved the standing of students in the United States, Australia, and England in international assessment programs, nor have they narrowed the achievement gaps among different groups of children (Zhao, 2018b). The reforms have not led to more engagement, more positive social and psychological experiences, or more confident and happy students in Asian schools (OECD, 2017; Zhao, 2018e).

There have also been serious efforts to better prepare children for the changed and changing world. Many governments have introduced 21st century skills or other new capabilities, such as global competency and entrepreneurial thinking, into their curricula (Australian Curriculum Assessment and Reporting Authority, 2010; European Parliament & Council of the European Union, 2006; Zhao, 2015a). But the majority of schools offer the same education experiences for all children. As a result, as Tony Wagner, a well-known thought leader in education, points out in his book, there is a global achievement gap, the gap between what schools teach and what the world needs, because even our best schools do not teach the new survival skills (2008).

Wrong Fixes

The failure of these reforms to improve education is not surprising, but the reason is not that these efforts did not have an impact on schools due to the usual reasons of resistance and inertia (Tyack & Cuban, 1995; Tyack & Tobin, 1994). On the contrary, these reforms have significantly affected curriculum, school staff, and school culture, as exemplified by the sweeping changes brought about by the No Child Left Behind Act to American schools (Zhao, 2018e).

The reforms failed because they did not address the root cause of the problems: the traditional education paradigm (Zhao, 2012, 2018a, 2018b). In other words, the reforms were designed to strengthen the very apparatus that is the cause of the problems. Thus, instead of solving the problems, the reforms exacerbated them.

Prescribed Skills and Knowledge

The traditional paradigm of education starts with the assumption that all children need the same set of skills and knowledge to succeed in adult life, and all children are capable of and interested in acquiring the same skills and knowledge. Thus, we have curriculum standards and grade-level expectations to codify what and when children need to learn and tests to verify that they have learned the prescribed skills and knowledge.

Teacher- and Adult-Directed Learning

Conventional education further assumes that children must be explicitly taught and managed by adults. Thus, we have them organized into classes monitored by adults and carefully structure their time into manageable segments.

Uniform Instructional Methods

Furthermore, the traditional paradigm of education assumes that all children learn the same way and progress at a similar pace. Thus, we have uniform instructional methods and arrange children into grades based on their biological ages.

Grades and Exams

Finally, the traditional paradigm operates as a mechanism to sort students into different positions and award different opportunities and resources based on the extent to which they have mastered the prescribed skills and knowledge. Thus, we have grades and exams.

Some elements of the prevailing education paradigm may have been more or less valid in the Industrial Age (Zhao, 2012, 2016b, 2018c), but no longer. Nonetheless, this paradigm is the very cause of the problems leading to the widespread dissatisfaction with education today. First, not everyone needs the same set of skills and knowledge to succeed in adult life, except for a small set of basics. In today's world, what makes one successful is a combination of personal qualities and skills unique to each individual (Zhao, 2018b, 2018c). However, this outdated assumption directly leads to the so-called achievement gaps because not every child has the same resources, environments, capacities, and interests that help them acquire the same skills and knowledge at the same pace.

Second, when children are forced to learn things they are not interested in or find irrelevant, they become bored and disengaged. When they are constantly being seen as failures, they become frustrated and disengaged. When they are pitted against each other to compete for higher scores on the same tests, they become anxious and experience unhealthy social relationships. When they are deprived of ownership and autonomy, they become less motivated and engaged. The Gallup Student Poll shows a gradual decline in engagement as grades go up, with students in primary grades most engaged (2017), suggesting that as students spend more time with the one-size-fits-all paradigm of education and they become more autonomous, they become less engaged.

Third, controlling what, when, how, and where children learn limits students' opportunities to develop the capabilities needed for success in today's world. As Engel points out:

> . . . our current educational approach doesn't just fail to prepare teenagers for graduation or for college academics; it fails to prepare them, in a profound way, for adult life.
>
> We want young people to become independent and capable, yet we structure their days to the minute and give them few opportunities to do anything but answer multiple-choice questions, follow instructions, and memorize information. We cast social interaction as an impediment to learning, yet all evidence points to the huge role it plays in their psychological development. (Engel, 2011)

Time for Something Different

"The definition of insanity is doing the same thing over and over again and expecting a different result." Although Albert Einstein probably did not come up with this witty and insightful quote that has often been (mis-)attributed to him (Becker, 2012), the message remains powerful.

We cannot repeatedly do the same thing to improve education and expect a different result. It is time to try something totally different.

That's what the Independent Project did. The Independent Project represents a complete departure from the traditional paradigm. It rejected the idea that all children should learn the same skills and knowledge codified in curriculum standards. Instead of forcing students to follow a curriculum, the Independent Project enabled them to design and develop their own curriculum. The project dismissed the belief that students must be explicitly taught by adults. Although they consulted with teachers, students managed and organized the learning on their own. The project also abandoned the idea that all children make similar progress and need to be grouped by biological age. Students in the Independent Project were from different grade levels and ages and they worked with each other very well. Furthermore, the Independent Project did not include exams or grades. Instead, the students evaluated each other.

The Independent Project exemplifies a new paradigm of education. This paradigm does not presuppose or predefine what knowledge or skills children should and must learn. In this paradigm, the "curriculum" is one that follows the child. It begins with the children: what they are interested in, what excites them, what they are capable of, and how they learn. This paradigm does not assume all children are the same; therefore, it does not impose artificial standards or age-based, grade-level expectations. It helps children move forward from where they are. Furthermore, it does not believe children are simply empty vessels ready to be filled with knowledge, but rather it assumes that each child is a purposeful agent who interacts with the outside world.

The difference between conventional education, or the old paradigm, and the new one is best summarized by the American educator and philosopher John Dewey in his book *Experience and Education*:

> To imposition from above is opposed expression and cultivation of individuality; to external discipline is opposed free activity; to learning from texts and teachers, learning through experience; to acquisition of isolated skills and techniques by drill, is opposed acquisition of them as means of attaining ends, which make direct vital appeal; to preparation for a more-or-less remote future is opposed making the most of the opportunities of present life; to static aims and materials is opposed acquaintance with a changing world (Dewey, 1938, pp. 5–6).

The new paradigm is not really new. Even before Dewey, great education thinkers, such as Swiss education reformer Johann Heinrich Pestalozzi and Genevan philosopher Jean-Jacques Rousseau, articulated similar ideas underlying the paradigm. These ideas have also been put into practice in democratic schools for a long time. For example, schools like Summerhill (Neil, 1960; Stanford, 2008), Sudbury Valley School (Greenberg, Sadofsky, & Lempka, 2005), and Jefferson County Open School (Posner, 2009) have followed these ideas for decades.

But these ideas have never entered mainstream public education. Their practice has often been confined to a very small number of schools, mostly private and small scale. And these schools are generally seen as too radical for the masses. As a result, policymakers have been unwilling to consider these ideas for an entire education system, and few traditional schools have been willing to embrace these beliefs and replace the traditional paradigm with the new one. It seems that we have arrived at a time when these ideas are needed for every child.

The key to realizing the new paradigm of education is student ownership. In the Independent Project, students owned their education. As owners, they took control of what they wanted to learn and how they wanted to learn. They also owned their education environment. They made decisions about whom they wanted to work with. They also made decisions about how to organize and manage their learning as a community. Having ownership is perhaps the most important factor that led to the success of the Independent Project, as pointed out by Engel in her *New York Times* piece:

> The students in the Independent Project are remarkable but not because they are exceptionally motivated or unusually talented. They are remarkable because they demonstrate the kinds of learning and personal growth that are possible when teenagers feel ownership of their high school experience, when they learn things that matter to them, and when they learn together. In such a setting, school capitalizes on rather than thwarts the intensity and engagement that teenagers usually reserve for sports, protest, or friendship.

Accepting that students are the owners of their education is to recognize and respect students' right to self-determination. Students, however young they may be, are human beings. And human beings in many countries have the right to self-determination, including self-determination over their own education. It is unfortunate that this right has been taken away from children, ironically in the name of giving them an education. For the sake of a better education for all children and a better world for everyone, we need to return this right to our children.

The Independent Project shows one way to return the right to self-determination over education to children. In this book, we combine our years of experience in teaching entrepreneurship and creativity and in individualizing instruction to promote self-determined learning to lay out a path that leads to a new direction and that places the missing actor in education—the student—back into the educational picture.

Why Student Ownership and Self-Determined Learning

Many young children hate vegetables. If you are a parent, it is a situation that has probably frustrated you. If you are not a parent, it is something that probably frustrated your parents! Green, orange, boiled, stewed, steamed, raw . . . it doesn't matter. Many children simply will not eat vegetables, no matter how many times you explain that they are good for their growing bones, how many ways you try to bribe them, or how many clever ways you disguise them.

A research team in Spain—where they love their meals—conducted an experiment with 150 4- to 6-year-old children. These children were surveyed to determine their preferences from among the six most commonly eaten vegetables in Spain. Eventually, two—zucchini and green beans—were selected because they were neither at the top of most children's preferred vegetable list nor at the bottom.

The experiment was run in the lunch cafeteria at each child's elementary school. Carefully weighed portions of zucchini and green beans were placed on the typical school cafeteria plates. Children came to the serving line, picked out a vegetable, and sat down to eat, just as they did every school day.

They had, however, been randomly divided into three groups. One third were assigned to a condition in which they did not get to choose which vegetable they received: they were randomly handed either a plate of zucchini or a plate of green beans. Another third of the children had the opportunity to choose either the zucchini or the green beans. A third group could choose either the zucchini or the green beans and could go back to the lunch line and get a helping of the other vegetable if they desired. All the children were told to eat as much or as little as they wanted and that if they wanted more, they could come and get more (of the same vegetable for the first two groups, of either vegetable for the third group). The researchers weighed the total grams of vegetables consumed by each child.

The results? The children in both choice groups consumed more than twice the weight of zucchini and green beans as did the children in the no-choice group (Dominguez et al., 2013).

Choice. It is, apparently, stronger than a child's aversion to vegetables.

Self-Determination

Freedom, Liberty, and Self-Determination

The freedom to choose is not only a way to help children eat more vegetables but, more importantly, the rights to life, liberty, and the pursuit of happiness are inherent and inalienable as enshrined in the U.S. Declaration of Independence, and the right to freedom for all humans is affirmed in the United Nations (UN) Universal Declaration of Human Rights. All humans include children. Thus, children should have the same inherent and inalienable rights: life, liberty, and the pursuit of happiness. Unfortunately, children are frequently denied the right to liberty in the name of education. The right to liberty can be interpreted to include the right to self-determination: the freedom to make choices and take actions without external coercion.

Article 12 of the UN Convention on the Rights of the Child requires that: "States Parties shall assure to the child who is capable of forming his or her own views the right to express those views freely in all matters affecting the child, the views of the child being given due weight in accordance with the age and maturity of the child" (United Nations, 1989).

But educational institutions often coerce, overtly and covertly, children into behaviors and actions without consulting the child. Today, children have little liberty over what they do in school and how and when they do it and, ultimately, what kind of person they want to become. The curriculum is predetermined; the delivery of the curriculum is predetermined; the setting is predetermined; and the assessment is predetermined. No wonder they are bored. It seems self-evident that children prepared in this "other-determined" manner will be poorly equipped to navigate an adult world requiring that they act autonomously and self-determine learning to acquire skills in rapidly changing environments.

All of this is done in the name of education, of preparing children to become successful individuals. In other words, the violation of children's right to freedom is done for "their own good." It is carried out under the assumption that children are too immature to know what's good for them or incapable of acting in their own interests. Or because they don't know what's worth learning or are unwilling or unable to learn what's worth learning.

Research shows that none of these reasons are valid. Children are born learning machines. Learning is central to human survival. Children want to learn and can learn. They can also organize and manage their own learning. Research also shows that authoritarian parenting and education that deprives children of the right to self-determination is harmful for learning. When children are deprived of the opportunities, they disengage, lose agency, develop low self-efficacy and antisocial behaviors, and possibly lose interest in exercising their self-determination. As a result, they become dependent on others to make choices for them.

Self-determination is more than a right, however. More than a century of theory and research in psychology and special education has emphasized the importance of individual or personal self-determination; not the right to self-determination, but the importance of motivations and qualities that enable young people to act volitionally and make things happen in their own lives. What does it mean to be self-determined? When young people are self-determined, they

- Are the actors in their own lives; they make or cause things to happen in their lives, rather than other people or circumstances making or causing them to act in other ways.
- Are autonomously motivated to seek opportunities and experiences that enable them to reach personal goals that improve their life satisfaction and to shape their world to improve their lives.
- Become more engaged and active in learning and in maintaining positive mental health, rather than being passive and anxious.

Ultimately, to effectively prepare young people to meet the demands of the 21st century, schools must replace historic practices with practices that foster student ownership over education and promote self-determined learning. In this chapter, we'll explore self-determination as motivation to understand the "why" of self-determined learning. In Chapter 3, we'll look at self-determination as causal agency to better understand the "how" of self-determined learning.

Humans Are Motivated to Be Self-Determining

As educators, we want to enable students to become self-motivated and engaged. Self-determined young people act autonomously and are self- (or intrinsically) motivated. One of the most powerful ways of understanding autonomous motivation is through Self-Determination Theory (SDT), introduced by Richard Ryan and Edward Deci, two of the most influential motivational psychologists in the last half century. The following Research and Theory section provides a closer examination of SDT.

Research and Theory: Self-Determination Theory

Self-Determination Theory (SDT) differentiates motivation into autonomous and controlled types: essentially intrinsic or extrinsic motivation. SDT is "centrally concerned with the social conditions that facilitate or hinder human flourishing" and "critical inquiries into factors, both intrinsic to individual development and within social contexts, that facilitate vitality, motivation, social integration, and well-being . . . " (Ryan & Deci, 2016, p. 3).

SDT proposes that people are motivated to act to meet three basic psychological needs: *autonomy*, *competence*, and *relatedness*. Action to meet these three basic psychological needs energizes the development of autonomous motivation, consisting of intrinsic motivation (doing an activity because it is enjoyable) and/or internalized extrinsic motivation (doing an activity because it leads to a valued consequence separate from the activity itself) (Deci & Ryan, 2012, p. 88). SDT explains why people act in ways that are based on internal factors such as interests, preferences, values, and beliefs and in pursuit of valued goals. Efforts to fulfill basic psychological needs of autonomy, competence, and relatedness energize people and are linked to maintaining autonomous (intrinsic) motivation.

Autonomy. SDT uses the term autonomy for different purposes: as an optimal motivational state (e.g., autonomous motivation) and as a basic psychological need.

> To be autonomous means to behave with a sense of volition, willingness, and congruence; it means to fully endorse and concur with the behavior one is engaged in. (Deci & Ryan, 2012, p. 85)

The basic psychological need for autonomy is satisfied when a person experiences choice and volition. Autonomous actions are self-endorsed and congruent with one's values and interests (Vansteenkiste, Niemiec, & Soenens, 2010).

Competence. The basic psychological need for competence refers to a person's need to be effective within environments. The psychological need for competence motivates people to engage in actions that are challenging and to persist at such actions until successful. This need does not refer to skills or skill levels but to one's *perceptions of competence and mastery in one's environment*, to the experience of perceiving increased mastery and effectiveness (Deci, Ryan, & Guay, 2013; Sheldon, Ryan, & Reis, 1996).

continued

Research and Theory: Self-Determination Theory (*continued*)

Relatedness. The final basic psychological need is for relatedness, which refers to the need for people to feel connected with others and to feel a sense of social belonging. It refers not to physical relationships but to the feeling that one belongs, is cared for, and is connected (Hofer & Busch, 2011).

SDT proposes that the fulfillment of basic psychological needs for autonomy, competence, and relatedness leads to autonomous motivation.

Children are born learners; they are naturally curious and seek to explore their environments and understand themselves and others. And, according to SDT, humans are moted to be self-determining. Our role, as educators, is to establish the context in which students can self-determine learning.

The NU Not-School

These basic psychological needs, not simply abstract, theoretical constructs, can be put into play in how we structure schools to achieve student ownership and self-determined learning. In Iceland, a school for 8th to 10th grade students who are passionate about sports is structured around basic psychological needs; the school environment, structure, curriculum, and staff training are centered around providing autonomy supports, competence supports, and relatedness supports. The school is called NU, which is Icelandic for NOW. It is not the NU *School*, because founder Kristjan Omar Bjornsson and his faculty don't think of this as school, at least in the traditional sense. They see it as a workplace for growth. The day starts in accordance with students' biological clocks; there is no set timetable, but instead, student days are guided by individualized programs and sequences. There is no homework, few specified subjects, not many books, no traditional classrooms, and only a few chairs and tables. Standing desks and yoga mats are scattered about.

University of Iceland researcher Ingibjorg Kaldalóns has studied NU, for despite its nontraditional approach, the students at NU still have to complete the national curriculum and take obligatory standardized tests. Kaldalóns documented how the NU faculty and structure support autonomy, competence, and relatedness.

Autonomy supports take the form of meaningful student choices about almost every element of the day, from when and what to work on, where to go, when to start and stop, and who to work with. Students are supported to self-initiate action toward these choices. There are *Passion*

Hours every week in which students engage in whatever their passion is; and there are *Now-Being Sessions* that encourage student self-reflection and self-awareness. Every student has an individualized learning plan, and work is identified that is relevant to the student's interests, preferences, values, and beliefs. The faculty and staff eschew controlling features of typical schools, and students are part of rule setting and governance. They take ownership over their learning and their learning environment.

Finding a child's passion is an important element of promoting autonomy. We mentioned that NU attracts students who are passionate about sports. The learning activities relate to this passion. Kaldalóns, the Icelandic researcher studying NU, observed that when students were studying science, the lesson was about movement, and it was all connected to sports. When teaching English, Kaldalóns observed, they chose books and learning materials about sports. And movement is a part of the daily routine as well, not just studying it! Every hour students take time for some movement—handstands or exercise—and they then change working positions from standing to sitting, from sitting to laying on a mat. And the *Now-Being* sessions are focused on sports-related goals, using mindfulness and meditation to visualize achieving such goals.

Competence supports are provided by emphasizing mastery experiences: student challenges are matched to student abilities so that every student can master some aspect of the content. Assessment is used to provide feedback, not evaluation. Students are acknowledged for the goal process and not just goal outcomes. Materials and content are matched to student strengths and interests.

And relatedness supports take the form of four-day retreats every fall when students, faculty, and staff stay together and share common experiences. Teachers communicate with students in positive, encouraging ways, recognizing effort and progress. Students go through exercises in teamwork and community building with their peers and the faculty.

The NU is new, quite literally. It is too early to determine its long-term success. But ask any student there: they are not bored, and they are passionate about their "work."

That, most educators would agree, is most of the battle won!

Thoughts on Autonomy and Choice

In self-determined learning, teachers teach and support students to teach themselves. Learners are highly autonomous, and the teacher relinquishes ownership of learning to the learner. So what, exactly, does "relinquishes ownership of learning to the learner" imply? It certainly can't mean that students are set adrift to learn by themselves with no support or direction. Nor can it mean that teachers have no ownership in the education process themselves. Self-determined learning emphasizes autonomy and choice, and it is worth taking a deeper dive into what we mean by these words to get a richer understanding of self-determined learning.

Independence Versus Dependence

When most people think of the word *autonomy*, they think of it as meaning independence. Automobiles that drive independently are autonomous vehicles. In child development, we often talk about the transition from adolescence to young adulthood as reflecting greater autonomy and independence; no longer being "dependent" upon one's parents. Autonomy-as-independence contrasts with dependence. The values of freedom and independence are ingrained in our society and many others.

Saying that in self-determined learning students are highly autonomous is not exactly the same as saying that students are independently directing learning. Certainly, self-determined learning implies that educators teach students to learn as independently as possible. Teachers arrange environments that promote choice and emphasize student direction in learning. We'll talk about these strategies more in a subsequent chapter, but there are also limitations to considering self-determined learning as simply synonymous with independent learning.

What if students have difficulty learning on their own? Aren't there subjects and topics that only someone with knowledge about that topic or subject can teach a student? What if students don't want to learn what teachers know they need to learn? Won't students think that what they have to learn is boring and just do something they think is fun? There are lots of reasons that students may choose not to learn something that is not inherently enjoyable. And yet, we know as adults that learning such things may enable them to reach outcomes that are enjoyable and important, which is why we need to go beyond thinking about autonomy as only, or even mainly, independence.

Volition Versus Pressure

There is another way to think about autonomy other than independence. Think back to how SDT uses autonomy. In *Autonomy in Adolescent Development: Toward Conceptual Clarity*, Belgian psychologist Bart Soenens and colleagues observed that

When people are autonomously motivated, they engage in an activity willingly. This is because the activity is inherently satisfying and interesting (i.e., intrinsic motivation) or because people see the personal value of engaging in the activity. . . . Thus, even when an activity is not inherently enjoyable or challenging, people can still internalize its importance, thereby experiencing greater ownership over the behavior and displaying autonomous motivation. (Soenens, Vansteenkiste, Van Petegem, Beyers, & Ryan, 2018, p. 5)

There's that word again—ownership—but in relation to actions that are not inherently enjoyable. Like eating vegetables?

Understanding autonomy-as-volition gives us a way to think about self-determined learning without the conflicts that autonomy-as-independence introduce. We turn over ownership for learning to students by supporting them in engaging in activities that are of personal value to them and to act volitionally. Soenens and his colleagues observed that

Independence is mainly about the question of how much adolescents depend on others and who is regulating a certain behavior or goal (i.e., the parent, the adolescent, or both). In contrast, volitional functioning is more about within-person concordance; that is, about the degree to which behaviors or goals are aligned with one's deeply held values, preferences, and interests. (p. 6)

Volition is a word that is a bit like *autonomy*. We think we know what it means, but when we look at it with greater scrutiny, its meaning is richer. We think of *volition* as simply acting based upon preferences or interests. But look at any definition of the word, and you get a slightly different take. Volition is acting based on conscious choice. Conscious implies awareness and intentionality. When students act volitionally, they act based on preferences and interests but do so intentionally. Intentional action is, implicitly, goal-oriented, and thus, *volitional action* implies the pursuit of goals based on one's preferences and interests. The activities leading to that goal may not, in and of themselves, be personally enjoyable, but the goal itself is valued and based on one's interests and preferences.

Sitting in a seat for four hours at a concert by an artist you have long wanted to see is different than sitting in a seat for four hours during a training to get continuing education credits to keep your teaching license. However, they are both acts of volition. Attending the concert was inherently satisfying and enjoyable in itself. Completing the inservice training was not necessarily enjoyable, but it had personal value and relevance, and thus it was in service to the larger goal of your career as a teacher.

Autonomy-as-independence and autonomy-as-volition are not completely distinct and nonoverlapping concepts. Soenens and colleagues pointed out that "situations of independence provide relatively more room for volitional functioning, possibly because such situations provide more opportunity for expressing one's personal preferences, values, and interests in these situations" (p. 7).

Thus, autonomy means volitional action in which students assume ownership over their learning; when they are motivated to learn because the learning task or objective is enjoyable to them (i.e., intrinsically motivating) or because the learning provides an opportunity for the expression of and is aligned with students' personal preferences and values. They see the personal value to engaging in the activity, even if the activity is not particularly enjoyable or challenging.

Autonomy is a nuanced construct. Surely, though, choice must be fairly straightforward. Choosing is just selecting among options (like zucchini or green beans), right? You know it's not that simple, and understanding that complexity will, again, help you understand what we mean by self-determined learning.

Choice and Autonomy

Think about how you use the word "choice" (or choose) in daily language. For instance, a mobile phone company offers greater choice. We have to live with the choices we make. There are too many breakfast cereals to choose from. The right to choose is a fundamental American value.

You probably don't need it pointed out that all of these uses of "choice" mean something slightly different.

Psychologists who study choice suggest three processes subsumed under that idea of choice. First, there is the degree to which context affords someone the opportunity to choose; mobile phone companies offering choice and our right to choose as a citizen reflect this meaning of choice as referring to the context. Second is the actual act of a person selecting from among two or more options; this is the physical act of making a selection . . . of choosing.

Psychologists are interested in mental aspects of behavior, so the third process is *perceived choice*, which refers to the "subjective experience of having opportunities to make choices, options to choose among, and the experience of freedom while choosing" (Patall & Hooper, 2018, p. 151).

The act of choosing is almost always contingent on the availability of choice (i.e., options), so let's group those two together for our purposes and look more closely at choosing and perceived choice.

Choosing. Choosing is the act of making a choice; the selection of one option over other options. It is what was, at the surface, studied by the Spanish researchers who revealed the magic of choice and children's vegetable intake. Choosing is an action associated with the idea of autonomy-as-independence, but it is also linked with autonomy-as-volition. Research has shown that "providing students with task-related choices leads to enhanced feelings of autonomy (volitional functioning), interest, enjoyment, and persistence on a task and to enhanced task value, effort, engagement, performance, subsequent learning, and perceived competence" (Patall & Hooper, 2018, p. 153).

But is it simply the actual act of choosing that is most important here? Not always. When confronted with a grocery store aisle of breakfast cereal boxes, choosing not only doesn't seem autonomy enhancing, it feels like a burden. Or most of us can relate to the notion of a Hobson's choice . . . choosing from only one option. Reverend Hobson was a 16th century stable owner in Cambridge, England; in fact, he was the only stable owner in that university city on the River Cam. The good reverend had a stable full of horses, but in reality, customers could only select the horse in the first stall. You guessed it: that horse was a nag. In later years, a Hobson's choice came to refer not only to a "take this or nothing" choice but also choosing from among options that are all bad.

In fact, one element of why the act of choosing promotes autonomy, competence, and engagement is that the person *perceives* the choice as promoting "a sense of freedom to express one's preferences and initiate or regulate one's own behavior" (Patall & Hooper, 2018, p. 156). It is doubtful that the Reverend Hobson's parishioners ever perceived their "choice" as in any way volitional! The perception of choice is as important as the act of choosing.

Perceived choice. What factors regulate whether we perceive a choice to be autonomy enhancing or controlling? It is not just the significance of the choice that matters. Trivial choices have been shown to promote autonomy. Nor is it just that the choice is from something interesting. Quite the opposite, in fact. Research suggests that infusing choice options into tasks that are not intrinsically motivating creates a greater sense of autonomy-as-volition than choices among already interesting activities. In the former, boring, mundane, or tedious tasks become more autonomy enhancing because you express your preferences, values, and interests in the choice opportunity. In the latter, your interests, preferences, and values are already being expressed, so adding in a choice doesn't change much.

Think about the vegetable experiment. Children who had more choices ate more because their choice opportunities allowed them to insert some preference and interest in an activity that was, in and of itself, not highly preferred. Had the experiment been on consumption of ice cream, it is unlikely the choice element would have impacted how much ice cream the children in the three groups ate.

Marketing professionals know something about how choice motivates us. In a series of linked studies, researchers at the University of Michigan examined the factors that actually made the act of choosing more satisfying to coffee-drinking college students. The researchers varied a choice or no-choice condition (e.g., what cup of coffee the participant drank) with a high-differentiability versus low-differentiability condition; that is, high or low differences in the attributes of the coffee like fruitiness, fermentation and body, floral scent, and so forth. They then measured satisfaction with the coffee the person drank (either chosen independently or randomly assigned a cup to drink). When there were low levels of differentiation among the blends, nonchoosers were as satisfied with what they drank as were choosers. When there were high levels of differentiation, however, choosers were much more satisfied than nonchoosers (Botti & McGill, 2006).

In other words, if choice options are not *meaningfully* different, making choices does not promote autonomy. If it was simply the act of choosing that led to the sense of autonomy-as-volition, that would not be the case. That it is the case suggests that we attribute choices that are meaningful to be an expression of ourselves. Research shows that coerced choices do not promote autonomy, competence, or engagement.

A study by University of Southern California researcher Erika Patall shows how these issues impact another often-contentious element within schools: homework.

High school students taking chemistry, world history, government, psychology, and earth science classes were randomly assigned to either a choice or no-choice condition with regard to how homework was assigned. High schoolers in the choice condition could select from two similar homework assignments to complete. For each student in the choice condition, a student in the no-choice condition was assigned the same assignment, so an equal number of each homework assignments were completed by students in both conditions. Instructions to complete the homework assignment and deadlines to turn in the assignment were the same for all students. Eventually, students in the no-choice and choice conditions switched conditions and the process was implemented again.

When students had a choice of homework, they reported more intrinsic motivation (autonomy) to complete the homework and higher levels of perceived competence in completing the homework, and they performed better on the unit test examining the material.

Choosing . . . the magic elixir, right? Homework and vegetables.

But, there's more to the story. Patall and her colleagues also collected data on students' *perception* of the degree to which they were given choices by their teacher and the degree to which they perceived that their teacher was supportive of autonomy. Students' intrinsic motivation and perception of teacher autonomy supports were fully accounted for by their perception of receiving choices from teachers.

Choosing is important. But it is the perception of choice that makes such action supportive of autonomy. It is, in essence, a sense of ownership over the process, independent of the task, and the opportunity to infuse one's values, beliefs, interests, and preferences into even the most mundane tasks that matters. And it is meaningful differences in options that create ownership.

On Meaningfulness and Purpose

Meaningfulness is important in self-determined learning in more ways than just the choice-making process. Students who are bored (and who, as a result, perform poorly in school) frequently cite the meaninglessness of the work as an explanation for their boredom. Stanford University social psychologist William Damon, author of *The Path to Purpose: How Young People Find Their Calling in Life* (2008), stated that "More important than any particular behavioral signposts, such as tests passed, prizes won, or popularity gained, or even the general degree of happiness displayed, is the direction and meaning of a young person's efforts" (p. 37).

Teachers frequently voice concerns about the lack of motivation their students exhibit, but really, what is at play here? Students are highly motivated to do things they are interested in and enjoy doing. Is it that students are not motivated, or that school is not motivating?

Research in positive psychology and well-being has established that a strong predictor of well-being is a sense of meaning in life. Do meaning in life and meaning in activities matter? The Kelly Global Workforce Index, the largest of its kind in the world, collecting survey data on the workforce and workplace from around the world, found in its 2009 survey that more than half of workers, worldwide, would accept lower wages or take a lesser role if their work contributed to something that was important or meaningful (Kelly Services, 2009).

We've seen that choices that are perceived to be meaningful lead to a sense of autonomy and promote perceived competence. Why? Well, for one, when an activity is meaningful to us, we are more likely to pursue it, engage in it, and master it, leading to greater perceptions of autonomy, competence, satisfaction, and well-being. Psychologist Matthew Bundick put it this way:

> The degree to which an activity is seen as meaningful may reflect the degree to which engagement in that activity permits one to put into action one's talents and skills toward valued ends, and exercise mastery over one's environment. (2011, p. 58)

So, meaningfulness is linked to volition and perceptions of competence. As Bundick pointed out, a high school student may perform a community service activity because they want to and care about the cause or, alternatively, because they think they need to do so to have a good activity to put on a college application. The first is meaningful, and the second is not, even though the action may be identical. The result? Research in positive psychology shows that it is only when benevolent or prosocial acts are volitional and autonomously motivated that any benefit to well-being accrues (Weinstein & Ryan, 2010).

Finnish philosopher Frank Martela and researchers in SDT have studied meaningfulness and linked it to basic psychological needs for autonomy, competence, and relatedness. The satisfaction of all three basic psychological needs, along with a sense of benevolence, accounted for whether action was perceived as meaningful; in other words, when we act benevolently, we "satisfy the need for competence, insofar as one feels effective in helping; the need for relatedness, insofar as one feels more connected with others; and the need for autonomy, insofar as prosocial acts are volitional and autonomous" (Martela & Ryan, 2015, pp. 750–751). And, in turn, we feel that what we have done and who we are have meaning.

Self-Determined Learning and Student Ownership

So, with all this as prologue, why should educators embrace student ownership and self-determined learning? The Research to Practice section that closes this chapter summarizes the important elements of research and theoretical understanding for the "why" of student ownership and self-determined learning. In Chapter 3, we will explore the underlying research and ideas for the "how" of student ownership and self-determined learning.

Research to Practice: Why Student Ownership and Self-Determined Learning

Educational systems often predetermine the curriculum, instruction, and assessment because adults believe that children

- Are too immature to know what is good for them;
- Are incapable of acting in their own interests;
- Don't know what is worth learning; or
- Are unwilling or unable to learn what's worth learning.

But that is simply not true. Children are born learning machines who want to learn and can organize and manage their own learning. They are naturally curious and seek to explore their environments and understand themselves and others.

As educators, we harness these natural tendencies to motivate students to learn by promoting autonomy and choice. This does not mean that students are left alone to drift without structure and support. We turn over ownership for learning to the student by

- Supporting students to engage in activities that are of personal value to them and to act volitionally;
- Providing opportunities for students to choose and to see that their choices influence their education;
- Linking learning to meaningful activities; and
- Creating learning communities that emphasize student curiosity and experiences.

Why student ownership and self-determined learning? Because self-determined learning harnesses the power of student autonomy and student ownership over learning to motivate students to learn by

- Teaching students to teach themselves;
- Teaching students how to set and achieve goals and make plans;
- Creating learning communities and using teaching methods that emphasize students' curiosity and experiences;
- Ensuring that learning is tied to activities that are intrinsically motivating or lead to the attainment of goals that are valued and based on student preferences, interests, and values;
- Emphasizing mastery experiences, using assessments (both teacher-directed and student-directed) to provide supportive feedback, and aligning instruction with students' strengths and abilities; and
- Providing choice opportunities, supporting volition, and emphasizing the goal process and not just goal outcomes.

When these conditions are in place, students take the initiative in learning because learning is meaningful and of personal value to them. They act volitionally because they are provided choices that are meaningful, meaningfully different, and autonomy-supportive.

Promoting Student Ownership and Self-Determined Learning

Geelong is a thriving city in Victoria, Australia, about 75 miles southwest of Melbourne, along the road paralleling the coast of Port Phillip Bay. The city's name, derived from the language of the indigenous peoples native to that area, refers to the cliffs and stunning coastal landscape that make Geelong a tourist destination. In recent years, the city's name has also become associated with innovation in education. A school founded in the mid-19th century, the Geelong Grammar School, is one of the most innovative schools in Australia today and, indeed, in the world.

Geelong Grammar School serves more than 1,500 students from ages 3 to 18, some of whom live on campus, others of whom live at home. All the school's faculty and staff are trained to implement positive education, which is the application of positive psychology—hope, optimism, well-being, resilience, and so forth—to education. The school's model comprises six domains in which all activities are focused: *positive relationships, positive emotions, positive health, positive engagement, positive accomplishment,* and *positive purpose.*

One can easily find a commitment to student ownership and self-determined learning throughout the Geelong curriculum and structure. Several of these domains relate directly to the issues we discussed in Chapter 2: positive relationships emphasize social and emotional skills that foster relationships; positive engagement emphasizes the importance of student interest, passion, and curiosity; positive accomplishment emphasizes striving for outcomes that are meaningful to students; and positive purpose emphasizes contributing to others and the community, thus enhancing meaningfulness.

Geelong Grammar School has to meet the requirements of the Australian Government Department of Education and Training, as do all accredited schools in Australia, and its students perform well academically. In all grades in which students take the required National Assessment Program, which aligns with the Australian Curriculum, Assessment, and Reporting Authority requirements, 98.3 percent of students achieved at least national minimum standards in reading, writing, spelling, and numeracy (Geelong Grammar School, 2016), much higher than for schools in Australia on average. Annually, several graduating seniors earn the academically rigorous International Baccalaureate. These achievements are all the more impressive given that Geelong Grammar School has a nonselective enrollment policy, meaning that it accepts all students regardless of aptitude.

Although students at the Geelong Grammar School do well on tests and earn academic accolades, one gets the sense that this matters less, in some ways, than does students' performance on other youth outcomes measured at Geelong. A study by University of Melbourne researchers found that students at Geelong had more positive mental health and well-being outcomes (compared to students not at Geelong); felt more resilient and confident in their ability to achieve goals; used multiple well-being strategies to respond to everyday life events; were more hopeful; and reported higher levels of life satisfaction, happiness, gratitude, and perseverance (Vella-Brodrick, Rickard, & Chin, 2014). Young people who attend Geelong Grammar School succeed—the school uses the term *flourish*—through an education that emphasizes positive aspects of learning, harnesses student curiosity and interests, creates significant relationships, and links learning with purpose and meaningfulness. How can we, as educators, infuse these elements—with a focus on self-determination and self-determined learning—into every school and not just a few schools?

In this chapter, we provide an overview of the "how" of self-determined learning, including the importance of autonomy supports, competence supports, and relatedness supports. In Chapter 4, we'll explore in more depth how to provide enabling conditions for self-determined learning. In Chapter 5, we'll describe specific strategies that have been shown to facilitate self-determined learning.

Self-Determination as Causal Agency

We discussed self-determination as a right and self-determination as motivation in Chapter 2. Both uses of the term address *why* to promote self-determined learning. To understand *how* to promote self-determination, we need to explore yet another meaning of the term: self-determination as *causal agency*. The term self-determination, derived from centuries-old discussions in philosophy and psychology (see the Research and Theory section), is related to the questions of human agency.

Research and Theory: Self-Determination in Philosophy and Psychology

The idea of *self-determination* emerged in the Age of Reason in England in the 17th and 18th centuries. This was a time of ideas, revolutions, questioning authority, and of scientific breakthroughs and advances. It was in that cauldron of ideas about human freedom and human capacity to act and make changes that the idea of self-determination bubbled up. English Enlightenment philosopher John Locke coined the term in his influential *Essay Concerning Human Understanding,* published in 1690. Locke was addressing the *free-will* problem in philosophy.

Simply put, the free-will problem is a problem of *determinism*, which is the philosophical idea that "the past and the laws of nature together determine, at every moment, a unique future" (van Inwagen, 2008, p. 13). That is, our future actions are determined (caused) by our past and the laws of nature. For Locke and his followers, it meant that humans could make things happen in their own lives and that what one was and did was not predetermined.

In the 1930s, Andras Angyal, a founder of the field of personality psychology, proposed that an essential feature of human beings was their autonomy. Angyal (1941) observed that people live "in a world in which things happen according to laws which are heteronomous (i.e., governed from outside) from the point of view of the organism" and are "subjected to the laws of the physical world, as is any other object of nature, with the exception that it can oppose self-determination to external determination" (p. 33). Angyal applied the deterministic notion of Enlightenment philosophers to an understanding of how human beings act to influence their own lives.

Angyal's notions of self-determinism versus other-determinism influenced Deci and Ryan's theories of autonomous or intrinsic (versus extrinsic) motivation. The idea of self- versus other-caused action also propelled research and theory in applied disciplines, beginning with social work in the early 20th century, followed by education later in that century.

Agency

Agency refers to exerting power, and an agent is someone through whom power is exerted to achieve some outcome. You hire a real estate agent to exert power on your behalf to buy a home. Human agency refers to the power of people to act in their lives to achieve goals and attain desired outcomes. It "refers to the sense of personal empowerment involving both knowing and having what it takes to achieve goals," and theories of human agency view "people as active contributors to, or authors of their behavior, where behavior is self-regulated and goal-directed" (Wehmeyer, Little, & Sergeant, 2009, p. 357). In other words, theories that emphasize human agency view people as acting on their environments and in their lives through *agentic* actions such as solving problems, setting goals, and initiating action.

But it is important not to confuse agency with independent behavior or action (just like it was important not to confuse volition with independent action!). Harilyn Rousso, one of the nation's foremost advocates for women with disabilities, illustrates this with the story of her friend who is an artist. This woman, Connie, was born with Werdnig-Hoffmann disease, which resulted in only partial motor control of her arms and legs. Connie was driven by her passion for art to become an art therapist, despite that others questioned whether, because of her physical difficulties, she would be able to make art or to support others to make art.

Connie pursued her passion and created a successful career as an art therapist. For much of her life, she painted using an array of supports: a table easel that tilted; long handles to extend brushes, pens, or pencils; a hand grip to assist her in holding the adapted brush or pen; and a power wheelchair with a joystick to assist her in moving as she painted. As Connie got older, however, and painting became more difficult even with these accommodations, she came to rely more and more on an attendant who did some of these things for her, following Connie's instructions.

To people who questioned who the artist was, since Connie was not able to make the brush strokes completely on her own, Connie demonstrated that she could create identical pieces of art by giving directions to different assistants who could not see one another while she provided verbal instructions. It was her vision, artistic sense, and eye for color and design that created the art, not the physical act of applying paint to canvas. Connie said this about using another person as an attendant to support her:

> My attendant is an extension of my body. It takes a very emotionally as well as spiritually strong person to understand that and not resent it. If I don't direct the person, then I'm dependent on the person. Then I'm not autonomous and ultimately harder on the attendant. I make it very

clear that I'm not making decisions for them, only for myself. (Rousso, 1993, p. 111)

Agency and independent performance are not equivalent, just as autonomy-as-volition does not imply independent performance. Agency refers to action that enables people *to cause* things to happen in their lives.

Causal Agency

A team of researchers at the University of Kansas has formulated Causal Agency Theory (Shogren, Wehmeyer, & Palmer, 2017) as a means to describe the development of self-determination so as to inform attempts to design and evaluate efforts in schools to promote that development and greater youth agency.

Research and Theory: Causal Agency Theory

A *causal agent* is someone who makes or causes things to happen (self-determinism versus other-determinism) in their own life.

Causal Agency Theory views self-determined action as being energized by the basic psychological needs for autonomy, competence, and relatedness, as described by SDT. Motivations energize action. Efforts to act autonomously (volitionally) and fulfill basic psychological needs result in a causal action sequence. That causal action sequence consists of

- *Volitional actions.* The self-initiation of actions that enable one to set and pursue goals associated with one's preferences, interests, and passions.
- *Agentic actions.* Self-regulated and self-directed actions that enable one to progress toward freely chosen goals.
- *Action-control beliefs.* Beliefs that enable one to act with a sense of personal empowerment as an agent in one's learning and to take ownership over learning (Shogren, Wehmeyer, & Palmer, 2017).

Repeated experiences with this causal action sequence result in perceptions of oneself as a causal agent and, over time, in the development of self-determination.

Together, the Self-Determination Theory and Causal Agency Theory provide a framework for understanding how we create learning environments and deliver educational instruction. They can also be used to structure opportunities that promote student ownership, self-determination, and self-determined learning. They enable us to provide students with experiences like those of students at the Geelong Grammar School in Australia or the NU in Iceland.

Frameworks for Promoting Student Ownership and Self-Determined Learning

The question of importance becomes, then, what can we as educators do to make this a reality? In self-determined learning, teachers teach students to teach themselves. Students learn how to set and achieve goals and make plans, to be agents of their own learning. Teachers relinquish ownership for learning to the student, not by abdicating all roles in teaching but by creating learning communities and using teaching methods that emphasize students' curiosity and experiences. These methods are autonomy-supportive and ensure that learning is tied to activities that are intrinsically motivating or lead to the attainment of meaningful goals and that are based on student preferences, interests, and values. Teachers provide competence supports by emphasizing mastery experiences, using assessment (both teacher-directed and student-directed) to provide supportive feedback, and by aligning instruction with students' strengths and abilities. Teachers provide relatedness supports by providing choice opportunities, supporting volition, and emphasizing the goal process not just goal outcomes. Students take the initiative in learning because learning is meaningful and of personal value to them. They act volitionally because they are provided with choices that are meaningful, meaningfully different, and autonomy-supportive. Let's begin with this: what are the characteristics of autonomy-supportive teaching to facilitate student ownership and self-determined learning?

Autonomy-Supportive Teaching

The basic psychological need for autonomy is satisfied when a person experiences choice and volition. Autonomous actions are self-endorsed and congruent with one's values and interests (Vansteenkiste, Niemiec, & Soenens, 2010). Some of the characteristics of autonomy-supportive teaching include

- Recognizing students' strengths and abilities rather than limitations.
- Promoting students' volitional actions and perceptions of choice rather than dependency and pressure.
- Harnessing the power of students' passions and curiosity rather than conformity and standardization.
- Facilitating students' agency and ownership over learning rather than compliance and obedience.

- Creating value through meaningfulness and purpose rather than grades and tests.

Creating Autonomy-Supportive Contexts

Ask people what they picture when they think of a school classroom, and they will likely describe a room with chalkboards (or whiteboards if the person is younger), a few tall wooden cabinets to store teaching materials, a teacher's desk in the front or back of the room, a flag in a bracket on the wall near the door, perhaps a table with a lectern up front, windows providing a view of ballfields or the playground to stimulate daydreaming, and individual student desks lined up in rows facing the front of the room.

If there is a "traditional" room setup for education, that description is pretty close to it. One can see classrooms from the early 1900s that look, in layout, much like classrooms in the early 2000s. Some readers may remember, however, the Open Education movement from the late 1960s and 1970s: no walls, open spaces, and learning centers. Like other fads from the flower-power era that brought us puka-shell choker necklaces, streakers, and leisure suits, the Open Education movement fell out of fashion and walls were rebuilt, desks reordered, chalkboards remounted. Why? Well, teacher resistance for one thing. Open Education environments were loud, chaotic, and, according to critics, distracting. Education policy turned its focus in the 1980s and 1990s toward legislation and frameworks that emphasized standardized curricula, a focus on the basics, and high-stakes testing.

Is this what we mean by autonomy-supportive classrooms—no walls, no desks, and students going where they will and doing what they want? Well, yes and no. Stanford University Professor Emeritus Larry Cuban talked about the ebb and flow of beliefs about how schools are structured—traditional or, like schools without walls, progressive—in an issue of the Harvard Kennedy School Program on Education Policy and Governance e-zine, *Education Next*:

> Since children differ in their motivations, interests, and backgrounds, and learn at different speeds in different subjects, there will never be a victory for either traditional or progressive teaching and learning. The fact is that no single best way for teachers to teach and for children to learn can fit all situations. Both traditional and progressive ways of teaching and learning need to be part of a school's approach to children. Smart teachers and principals have carefully constructed hybrid classrooms and schools that reflect the diversities of children. Alas, that

lesson remains to be learned by the policymakers, educators, and parents of each generation. (Cuban, 2004)

Think about what the classrooms are like in NU. There, the Open Education influence is easy to see . . . few traditional desks, lots of standing desks, tables, or mats. Movement is part of the structure of the school. But not chaos. Why? When children are engaged in learning that is autonomously motivated, the chaos is replaced by intensity and engagement. But not every school has to be built without walls, doors, or hallways to promote autonomy. Classrooms in Geelong Grammar School are fairly traditional. Despite people remembering traditional classrooms (and blockbuster movies like *Dead Poets Society* reinforce those stereotypical images of classrooms), many classrooms in schools today, particularly at the elementary levels, are arranged with tables, learning centers, and reading areas—a hybrid of the traditional and the progressive advocated by Cuban. Essentially, autonomy-supportive classrooms are as much about *what the context supports* as they are about walls, doors, or desks.

In the Baldwin School District in Long Island, New York, administrators and teachers concluded that their traditional classroom arrangements were stifling opportunities for collaboration, creativity, and entrepreneurship. But instead of pursuing a one-size-fits-all approach, administrators invited teachers and students to submit ideas that might work for each classroom. Ann Marie Lynam's 7th grade social studies classroom was designed to accommodate her desire for mobility, flexibility, and diversity. Students come to her class with a wide array of abilities and experiences, from students who are academically advanced to students receiving special education services. The *Hechinger Report* described Lynam's classroom:

> The room has no "front," and everything is on wheels. A "genius bar," a la Apple stores, seats six students at a time at a raised, kidney-shaped table. The rest of the classroom's desks are arranged in groups to facilitate conversations on class assignments, and each group also has a comfortable ottoman or cushioned seat with a back to choose from. Sofas offer a final seating choice for students, whom Lynam trusts to make decisions that work best for them. (Mathewson, 2018)

In another classroom in the Baldwin district, kindergarten teacher Tricia Wilder opted for a theater nook that facilitates students acting out stories from books they read or lessons they learn. The classroom is replete with laptops, tablets for digital books, a touch-screen television, and, yes, a smartboard, all to facilitate greater student autonomy and self-direction.

The design has required that Wilder "relinquish some control" and "acknowledge that students can listen to a story while lying down on a couch instead of sitting cross-legged on a rug dutifully looking at the reader" (Mathewson, 2018).

Of the 17 redesigned classrooms in the Baldwin district, none are the same, but all embody features that emphasize choice opportunities, student self-direction, and student ownership of learning. Is the administration happy with the decision to redesign classrooms to enhance autonomy supports? Apparently so. They budgeted for 47 additional redesigns in one year.

So how can teachers structure learning environments to promote autonomy? Some basic principles are to

- Organize and design the classroom to maximize student active engagement and participation.
- Make needed materials or learning resources available for students to access easily.
- Create learning centers that emphasize various talents and preferences instead of just topics.
- Provide supports for all students to participate (e.g., digital books as well as print books, properly sized tables).
- Expressly provide spaces and structure where students can explore and pursue their passions.
- Ensure that students have meaningful roles in setting classroom rules and feel safe to explore and take risks.

The educational context is more than just the physical classroom, however. It is also the curricular and instructional materials with which students interact and to which they respond. Universal Design for Learning, or UDL, refers to a set of ideas and practices that turn the focus on the design and format of the curriculum, instructional materials, and the ways in which students demonstrate their knowledge and skills. UDL involves the design and use of materials that provide multiple means of engagement and offer options and features that promote student interest and self-regulation; provide multiple means of representing content through technology and pedagogy; and provide multiple means for students to respond to content (CAST, 2018).

Classrooms that embrace UDL utilize instructional materials that

- Provide choice options related to the level of difficulty or complexity of the material and activity and supports for learner self-direction (such as in Wilder's kindergarten class), and allow students to set learning goals.

- Provide options for exploration and experimentation and activities that are authentic, pertinent to real-world contexts, and have a clear purpose.
- Incorporate opportunities for self-evaluation and adjustment to the learning process to ensure success.
- Emphasize process and effort rather than just outputs and outcomes.

Universally designed materials provide multiple, flexible ways to display and deliver information, from providing multiple ways that content is represented (text, visuals, tabular information, figures, videos) to enabling students to control the speed at which content is presented, to providing text-to-speech. Learners are provided with opportunities through universally designed materials to self-regulate learning, monitor progress toward goals and objectives, and self-assess progress (CAST, 2018).

The fact is, all learners benefit from classrooms that embody UDL principles. Kyle Redford embraced UDL in her 5th grade classroom in Marin, California. She recognized the diversity of learners in her class and installed an amplification system in the class for a student who needed assistance to hear instructions and lectures. She discovered that other students in the class reported that the amplification helped them better follow and attend to instructions and explanations. Redford makes all written content available digitally, using text-to-speech apps on tablets, digital talking books, and audio readers from Bookshare.org, an accessible online library for students with visual impairments. Like the amplification system, Redford has found that quite a few of her students prefer to read along with the audio content or follow the captioned, highlighted words on the large television screen in the classroom. Students who have difficulty writing can dictate responses into devices, transcriptions of which help them see how they might structure a sentence (Redford, 2018).

And embracing UDL has changed Kyle Redford's use of assessment. In addition to written tests and quizzes (provided in alternative formats), she provides students with options to present information they have learned in other ways: through acting out what they've learned, performing a rap, or creating a movie using an iPhone. Redford says this about her experience:

> I have witnessed how my own (inexpert) shift toward UDL has helped all my students, not just the ones with the quirky learning profiles. Allowing students to access and express knowledge in multiple ways has allowed all abilities to more effectively optimize their strengths and minimize their weaknesses. (Redford, 2018)

Not all of these factors are in teachers' control. District and school policy, administrator actions, even federal policy all impact the capacity of teachers to create autonomy-supportive contexts. Without the administrative impetus, Baldwin School District teachers Lynam and Wilder would not have been able to redesign their classrooms. We'll return to that broader topic of enabling conditions for self-determined learning in Chapter 4. Now, though, let's turn to what it means to be an autonomy-supportive teacher.

Autonomy-Supportive Teachers

Autonomy-supportive teaching adopts the mantra that teaching is not steered by the textbook but by the needs and experiences of the learners. That sounds good, but how do we do that? Johnmarshall Reeve (2002) has studied the behaviors and interactions of autonomy-supportive teachers, concluding that

> . . . autonomy-supportive teachers distinguished themselves by listening more, spending less time holding instructional materials such as notes or books, giving students time for independent work, and giving fewer answers to the problems students face. (p. 186)

How you act toward students and how you respond to questions and provide answers are important. Reeve analyzed conversational statements of autonomy-supportive teachers, finding that they avoided directives, praised mastery, avoided criticism, gave answers less often, and responded to student-generated questions and communicating statements with empathy and perspective taking. He described the characteristics of autonomy-supportive teachers as being responsive, flexible, and motivating through interest.

Autonomy-supportive teachers

- Get to know the cognitive, social, and affective needs of each of their students.
- Create opportunities for students to get to know one another.
- Develop, maintain, and use a consistent and sustainable system of collecting information about individual student and group performance that will help them make informed grouping decisions throughout the year.
- Support students in how to work together for multiple outcomes.
- Understand and perform their role with learning groups as a coach, understanding the abilities and areas of needed support for each student.

- Ensure that every student, regardless of age or ability level, receives and talks about success and progress each day (Reeve, 2002).

Autonomy-Supportive Instruction

How teachers structure the educational context and how they interact with students are the first two elements of autonomy-supportive teaching. Providing autonomy-supportive instruction is the third. Some instructional strategies seem obvious. We know that promoting choice opportunities is important, and teachers can begin to do so by

- Incorporating options as to what activities students engage in to learn specific knowledge or content.
- Incorporating choice opportunities throughout a given activity.
- Increasing the number of contexts and domains in which choices are made.
- Raising the importance of choices students make in terms of consequences.
- Communicating with the students concerning areas of possible choice and the parameters within which options are available.

These are opportunities that are incorporated day in and day out at the Geelong Grammar School. In describing the principles of the school, Norrish (2015) noted that an "important teaching tool involves providing a level of choice between activities," which "encourages a sense of volition and supports students' need for autonomy" (p. 218). The faculty and staff at Geelong know that providing choice "also helps to create a match between challenge and skills level, as students can select an activity that suits their interests and perceived abilities" (p. 218). We'll see the importance of optimal challenges when we discuss competency-supportive teaching. One way that the structure of Geelong combines choice opportunities with a strengths-based approach is to allow students to choose from an array of workshops available on character strengths: students can choose a workshop that emphasizes their signature strengths or a strength they would like to enhance.

Steps to Self-Determined Learning

Columbia University Teacher's College professor Dennis Mithaug and colleagues have examined the theory and validity of self-determined learning from the context of promoting student engagement, as outlined in the following Research and Theory section.

Research and Theory: Self-Determined Learning Theory and Engagement

Mithaug and colleagues argue that research on factors associated with engagement indicate that learning is maximized when student engagement produces optimal experiences to new challenges (Mithaug, Mithaug, Agran, Martin, & Wehmeyer, 2003, p. 3). Let's unpack that so we can determine the elements of teaching self-determined learning. The basic propositions are

- When learners perceive that an opportunity for learning in a circumstance is valuable to them (e.g., self-endorsed and congruent with values, interests, and passions) and manageable . . . ; and
- When students have knowledge, beliefs, and experiences about their ability to self-regulate their actions to produce results (e.g., how to act as the causal agent in their lives) . . . ; then
- Students engage in the learning situations to optimize their adjustments and maximize their learning. (Mithaug et al., 2003, p. 3)

Recall the essential characteristics of causal action as leading to the development of self-determination suggested by Causal Agency Theory? These were volitional actions, agentic actions, and action-control beliefs. Mithaug and colleagues provide a framework to operationalize these theoretical constructs in which students

- Act to pursue personally valued learning outcomes with the expectations that they have the capacity to act as a causal agent and that if they do act, they can be successful (action-control beliefs);
- Self-regulate a problem-solving sequence to examine priorities based on preferences, interests, and values; prioritize the action needed to reduce the discrepancy between what is known and what needs to be known; set a goal to address that discrepancy (volitional action); and create an action plan to address the goal, design a self-monitoring process; and
- Implement the action plan, using information gathered through self-monitoring to evaluate progress toward the goal and adjust the action plan or goal as necessary to achieve the goal (agentic action).

Essentially, self-determined learning can be conceptualized as involving three steps, according to Mithaug and colleagues' analysis:

- Learners self-initiate action to set a goal and achieve a preferred outcome when that outcome aligns with self-interest and is congruent with their passions. That can be engagement in an activity that is intrinsically motivating in and of itself or an activity that is not particularly motivating itself but that leads to valued outcomes (remember the concert versus inservice training example from Chapter 2?).

- Learners self-regulate planning to create an action plan to address the goal and design a means to measure their own progress toward the goal.
- Learners use information they have gathered to self-evaluate progress and adjust their plan or goal, if necessary.

Research has established that "interventions designed to teach teachers how to support autonomy in their students result in higher student perceptions of autonomy supports" (Guay, Lessard, & Dubois, 2016, p. 96). Further, Guay and colleagues confirmed that the more that teachers implemented autonomy supports, the more engaged their students were in tasks. Research has clearly established that students' intrinsic motivation decreases from 3rd to 8th grade: year by year, steady as a funeral march. A large Canadian study confirmed that same progression for students ages nine to 15. But that study found something surprising. The trend slightly reversed after that age, with slight increases across time through age 18 (Gillet, Vallerand, & Lafrenière, 2012). Why? The trend in increased motivation was associated with the higher number of choices that students had in high school. Not enough to combat the boredom problem yet, but a promising finding.

Competency-Supportive Teaching

The second psychological need proposed by SDT is the need for competence, which refers to a person's need to be perceived as effective within environments. Students need to believe they are capable and competent. That seems self-evident, but does every child in your class feel that way? A norm-referenced, standardized education process essentially tells half of the students that they are below average, hardly a message that tells students they are competent. The psychological need for competence motivates people to engage in actions that are challenging and to persist at such actions until successful. As discussed in Chapter 2, this need does not refer to skills or skill levels but to one's perceptions of competence and mastery in one's environment, to the experience of perceiving increased mastery and effectiveness.

There are three things that research tells us as we think about promoting perceived competence, as outlined in the following Research and Theory section.

Research and Theory: Research in Promoting Perceived Competence

The majority of research in the basic psychological needs proposed by SDT has been with the basic need for autonomy. Ryan and Deci (2016) explained that this is "not that the need for autonomy is in any way more important than the needs for relatedness or competence" but that "in most settings, having support for autonomy as a contextual factor plays a critical role in allowing individuals to actively satisfy all of their needs" (p. 247). In essence, then, competency-supportive teaching is built on the foundation of autonomy-supportive teaching. When you establish contexts and engage in autonomy-supportive teaching and instruction, the groundwork is in place for competency-supportive teaching.

There are direct relationships between intrinsic motivation and optimal challenges that impact perceptions of competence. We've already seen that within a self-determined learning framework, learning is maximized when student engagement produces optimal experiences to new challenges. Research in SDT shows that intrinsically motivated people select optimal challenges (which occur in the context of autonomy supports or perceived autonomy) and "the experience of feeling competent when volitionally undertaking such tasks is what sustains intrinsic motivation over time" (Ryan & Deci, 2016, p. 153).

Additionally, performance versus mastery goals impact perceived competence differently. Mastery goals are those goals undertaken to improve one's knowledge, skills, or abilities. Performance goals are goals that tend to be comparative . . . looking at one's performance in contrast or comparison with others' performance (or a performance standard). Performance goals have been shown to improve academic performance, while mastery goals have been shown to improve academic performance and enhance well-being. What SDT adds to the equation is that when students set mastery goals that are autonomously motivated, the result is enhanced engagement and more positive learning outcomes (Ryan & Deci, 2016).

In addition to supporting autonomously motivated mastery goals, teachers provide competence supports by providing feedback that is similarly mastery based rather than norm-referenced, standard-based, or comparative.

Further, perceived competence is situated in autonomy-supportive contexts, teaching, and interventions. Students who are autonomously motivated to engage in optimal challenges that promote and are sustained by perceived competence, and supporting students to set mastery goals promotes autonomous motivation and enhanced competence. Mithaug and colleagues' theory of self-determined learning helps identify ways in which these findings from SDT fit into our framework for self-determined learning. Competence is enhanced when the following principles are implemented:

- Students engage when they have optimal opportunities to choose what they will do and how they will do it.

- Learning is maximized when student engagement produces optimal experiences to new challenges.
- Students stay engaged to the extent that they adjust their expectations, choices, and actions effectively enough to produce the gain that they expect.

What these principles emphasize is not just that optimal challenges promote engagement (through optimal opportunities to choose and, thus, as a function of autonomous motivation) but also that we need to provide learners with the adjustment skills that enable them to optimize challenges. Although one cannot know what the perfect level of challenge is in every learning circumstance, if we provide students with skills to adjust goals and plans according to their progress, they can self-regulate the adjustment process to identify an optimal challenge.

At the Geelong Grammar School, they operationalize these ideas to promote perceived competence using the philosophy behind both SDT and positive psychology founder Mihaly Csikszentmihalyi's Flow Theory (1991). Csikszentmihalyi explained the conditions resulting in optimal performance, which he called *flow* but which you might think of as "being in the zone" for learning and performance. Addressing the skill-challenge balance is an important element of Flow Theory and the Geelong approach. Students talk about the Goldilocks effect; that is, finding the challenge that is not too hard or too soft but just right. They work with faculty and peers to recall experiences in which their skills and challenges were well matched and to think about how that made them feel and how they figured out the match (Norrish, 2015).

One of the six domains of positive education implemented at Geelong Grammar School is the domain of positive accomplishments, defined as "the capacity to work toward meaningful goals, the motivation and grit to persist despite challenges and setbacks, and the achievement of competence and success in important life domains" (Norrish, 2015, p. 229). The Geelong positive accomplishment approach emphasizes meaningfulness and goal-oriented action, adjustment, and perceived competence embodied in self-determined learning.

In self-determined learning, a focus on competency-supportive teaching begins by implementing autonomy-supportive contexts, teaching, and instruction. Students are taught and supported to set and work toward mastery goals that result in both achievement and well-being, and teachers provide mastery-based feedback. A focus on strengths is capitalized on to create opportunities for optimal challenges, and students learn to adjust choices, expectations, and actions to reach goals.

Relatedness-Supportive Teaching

The final basic psychological need is for relatedness, which refers to the need for people to feel connected with others and to feel a sense of social belonging. It refers not to physical relationships but to the feeling that one belongs, is cared for, and is connected (Hofer & Busch, 2011). It probably doesn't take much to convince educators that relationships matter in education; for many of us, it is why we got into the field. But, then, we probably didn't get into the field to bore students, so perhaps we need to think a bit more about what we might be doing that either hinders or facilitates building feelings of connection and relatedness.

For one, when schools are structured around control, standardization, and compliance, among the first things to be impacted are trusting, meaningful relationships. In schools, "relatedness is deeply associated with a student feeling that the teacher genuinely likes, respects, and values him or her" (Niemiec & Ryan, 2009, p. 139).

Not surprisingly, relationships are a primary focus at the Geelong Grammar School. One of the school's six domains, as mentioned previously, is positive relationships. Students learn and practice forgiveness, gratitude, cooperation, communication, compassion, and trust. Faculty and students engage in a practice called "what went well," in which they share, either in a meeting or on a "what went well" bulletin board, positive and affirmative comments about one another. As a metaphor for the importance of relatedness, staff and students in the school use the Bucket-and-Dipper Theory forwarded by Donald Clifton, who developed the CliftonStrengths, and his grandson, Tom Rath, in their book *How Full is Your Bucket?* (2004). Every person has an (invisible) bucket that is either full or empty as a function of what people say or do to them. Every person also has a dipper that can be used to fill or empty others' buckets. At Geelong, children and staff hold the beliefs that:

> When buckets are full or overflowing, people feel happy, connected, and energized. When buckets are depleted, people feel miserable and exhausted. The dipper can be used either to fill other people's buckets or to dip from them. Examples of behaviors that fill a bucket include listening attentively, spotting strengths, and performing kind or thoughtful acts. Examples of behaviors that dip from a bucket include bullying, excluding others, or criticizing. (Norrish, 2015, p. 121)

As is the case with competency-supportive teaching, relatedness-supportive teaching builds on a foundation of autonomy-supportive teaching. Ryan and Deci noted that:

High-quality relationships are facilitated not only by having close and enduring social contacts with a partner but also by experiencing autonomous motivation within and for that contact. Autonomous motivation —that is, the individual's authentic willingness to participate in the relationship—contributes to high satisfaction and greater psychological wellness in both parties. (2017, p. 298)

That means, in essence, that when students perceive that teachers are autonomy-supportive, they are more likely to also believe that they (students) are cared for and cared about. The same is true for competency-supportive teaching; students who view themselves as more competent and capable and who view teachers as competency-supportive will also believe that they are cared for and cared about.

Relatedness supports involve more than creating a caring relationship between a student and a teacher; as at Geelong, relationships among students matter. In Ashley Coston Taylor's kindergarten class at Keene Elementary School in the Keene, Texas Independent School District, every student has a turn to serve as the class greeter. It is a way of telling every student that they belong. Each day, one of her students stands outside the classroom door at the beginning of the day and gives a handshake of welcome to every classmate as they come in. Recently, a video of one of Taylor's students, named Asher, went viral and even made *People* magazine! Asher is a young man with neurofibromatosis, a condition in which tumors form on the brain, resulting in impairments in communication, vision, motor skills, and growth. The video shows Asher, his backpack almost as big as he is, greeting his mostly taller classmates with a firm handshake. Periodically, one of his classmates steps in from the handshake to give Asher a hug, after which he returns to his handshaking responsibilities with gravity and focus (Hahn, 2018).

Asher didn't talk and had difficulty with fine motor skills. As he has begun to feel cared for and cared about—that he belongs—in Taylor's class, he has opened up, talking, feeling comfortable, and, importantly, feeling more confident.

Putting It All Together

Alice Macmillan is a 12th year student at Geelong Grammar School. All 12th year students do a project during the year. Not surprisingly, passion, meaningfulness, autonomy, and self-determined learning play a visible role in most of these students' projects. For Alice, it was a traumatic event in her family that spurred her passion and initiated her actions. Her older brother was diagnosed with epilepsy when Alice was in her 8th year. It was a severe seizure that resulted in her brother's hospitalization the summer before her 12th year, however, that ignited her passion to do her project on epilepsy awareness (Norrish, 2015).

To call what Alice did a school project is a bit like calling Yo-Yo Ma just a cellist. Her passion and the meaningfulness of the initiative motivated her to go well beyond preparing a paper or a demonstration. But first, she had to figure out what she wanted to do to act on that passion. Alice said that she "had so many ideas and was filled with ambition" (p. 213). To help her narrow down the path she would take, she surveyed her classmates to find out how much they knew about epilepsy. With those results in hand, she set a goal to educate her classmates about epilepsy and created a plan to do a video as the means to achieve that goal. She identified International Epilepsy Awareness Day and created posters to advertise the video and mark that date as a day of awareness at Geelong. Purple was the color associated with epilepsy awareness day, so the poster urged classmates to wear purple that day. Alice's efforts ended up going beyond just Geelong Grammar School. Through contacts she made with the Epilepsy Foundation, she was asked to be the junior ambassador for epilepsy in Victoria, a role that enabled her to take her passion-driven efforts to the whole community. She even convinced the local Australian Football League club, the Western Bulldogs, to include this in their media campaign (Norrish, 2015).

When International Epilepsy Awareness Day arrived, the Geelong Grammar School was awash in purple, all due to Alice:

> . . . my proudest moment was on Purple Day at Geelong Grammar School, seeing so many students dressed up in purple to support everything I had done. Everyone wanted to contribute, even in the smallest ways. Putting in so many hours and so much effort was all worth it in the end because of the amazing feeling I had in helping others and being selfless, of being positively engaged—and knowing that others were positively engaged alongside me. (Norrish, 2015, p. 214)

Alice's story illustrates the power and importance of self-determined learning. She felt amazing because her actions were volitional, meaningful, and purposeful; she felt competent and capable because she was able to reach a challenge; she felt that she was cared for and cared about because people supported her and were with her. Further, Alice's actions follow the framework for self-determined learning that we've discussed in this chapter.

How? Alice acted to pursue a personally valued learning outcome (increasing awareness of epilepsy) with expectations that she had the capacity to act as a causal agent to make or cause things to happen, and the belief that she could be successful. She engaged in self-regulated problem solving (surveying students) to determine the prioritized actions needed to reduce the discrepancy between what was known and what needed to be known and to set a goal (increase awareness of epilepsy in her school) to address that discrepancy, then created an action plan to address the goal (create a video, promote epilepsy awareness day), and designed a self-monitoring process (how much purple was seen on International Epilepsy Awareness Day). Alice implemented her plan and clearly reached her goal and beyond.

The Geelong Grammar School, with its focus on positive education, had clearly prepared Alice to be the causal agent in her own life. Is there any doubt that Alice will be successful in her life after Geelong Grammar School?

The Research to Practice section that closes this chapter summarizes the important elements of research and theoretical understanding for promoting student ownership and self-determined learning. We will return to a more practice-oriented look at strategies to promote self-determined learning in Chapter 5, but first, in Chapter 4, we will explore the enabling conditions that support student ownership and self-determined learning.

Research to Practice: Promoting Student Ownership and Self-Determined Learning

Human agency refers to the power of people to act in their lives to achieve goals and attain desired outcomes. In other words, theories that emphasize human agency see people as acting on their environments and in their lives through *agentic* actions such as solving problems, setting goals, and initiating action.

Agentic action is not, however, equivalent to independent action. *Agency* implies that people cause things to happen in their lives.

Educators foster student ownership and self-determined learning by ensuring autonomy-supportive teaching. Some of the characteristics of autonomy-supportive teaching include

- Recognizing students' strengths and abilities rather than limitations.
- Promoting students' volitional actions and perceptions of choice rather than dependency and pressure.
- Harnessing the power of students' passions and curiosity rather than conformity and standardization.
- Facilitating students' agency and ownership over learning rather than compliance and obedience.
- Creating value through meaningfulness and purpose rather than grades and tests.

continued

Research to Practice: Promoting Student Ownership and Self-Determined Learning (*continued*)

Principles for structuring the learning context to promote autonomy include

- Organizing and designing the classroom to maximize student active engagement and participation.
- Making needed materials or learning resources available for students to access easily.
- Creating learning centers that emphasize various talents and preferences instead of just topics.
- Providing supports for all students to participate (e.g., digital books as well as print books, properly sized tables).
- Expressly providing spaces and structure where students can explore and pursue their passions.
- Ensuring that students have meaningful roles in setting classroom rules and feel safe to explore and take risks.

Universal Design for Learning (UDL) involves the design and use of materials that provide multiple means of engagement that offer options and features that promote student interest and self-regulation; provides multiple means of representing content through technology and pedagogy; and provides multiple means for students to respond to content. Classrooms that embrace UDL utilize instructional materials that

- Provide choice options related to the level of difficulty or complexity of the material and activity and supports for learner self-direction, and allow students to set learning goals.
- Provide options for exploration and experimentation and activities that are authentic, pertinent to real-world contexts, and have a clear purpose.
- Incorporate opportunities for self-evaluation and adjustment to the learning process to ensure success.
- Emphasize process and effort rather than just outputs and outcomes.

Autonomy-supportive teachers

- Get to know the cognitive, social, and affective needs of each student.
- Create opportunities for students to get to know one another.
- Develop, maintain, and use a consistent and sustainable system of collecting information about individual student and group performance that will help them make informed grouping decisions throughout the year.
- Support students to work together for multiple outcomes.
- Understand and perform their role with learning groups as a coach, understanding the abilities and areas of support needed for each student.
- Ensure that every student, regardless of age or ability level, receives and talks about success and progress each day.

Autonomy-supportive instruction involves incorporating choice opportunities into day-to-day instruction by

- Incorporating options as to what activities students engage in to learn specific knowledge or content.
- Incorporating choice opportunities throughout a given activity.

- Increasing the number of contexts and domains in which choices are made.
- Raising the importance of choices students make in terms of consequences.
- Communicating with students concerning areas of possible choice and the parameters within which options are available.

Self-determined learning can be conceptualized as involving three fundamental steps:

- Learners self-initiate action to set a goal and achieve a preferred outcome when that outcome aligns with self-interest and is congruent with their passions.
- Learners self-regulate planning to create an action plan to address the goal and design a means to measure their own progress toward the goal.
- Learners use information they have gathered to self-evaluate progress and adjust their plan or goal, if necessary.

Competence is enhanced when the following principles are implemented:

- Students engage when they have optimal opportunities to choose what they will do and how they will do it.
- Learning is maximized when student engagement produces optimal experiences with new challenges.
- Students stay engaged to the extent that they adjust their expectations, choices, and actions effectively enough to produce the gain that they expect.

Relatedness-supportive teaching refers not to physical relationships but to the feeling that one belongs, is cared for, and is connected.

Students, when they perceive that teachers are autonomy-supportive, are more likely to also believe that they are cared for and cared about. The same is true for competency-supportive teaching: students who view themselves as more competent and capable and who view teachers as competency-supportive will also believe that they are cared for and cared about.

Enabling Conditions for Student Ownership and Self-Determined Learning

"When students are empowered to 'take charge' and control of their school journey, incredible things happen," said Luke Ritchie, principal of Annesley Junior School. The school, located near South Australia's capital city Adelaide, serves children from two years of age to 6th grade. While some may think the children are too young to take charge of their own learning, Luke has a different view: "We genuinely believe that children are capable now, not just in the future." This belief has put Annesley on a journey that "has been intentionally focused on increasing the levels of agency, autonomy, and self-determination."

Over the past few years, Ritchie and his colleagues at Annesley have been working on creating the enabling conditions for student ownership and self-determined learning. A key to this is a set of institutional arrangements that create space and infrastructure for students to exercise self-determination over their learning. These arrangements range from shared ownership that enables students to govern and decide on their learning environment, a broad and flexible curriculum that makes it possible for students to take control of their own learning paths, and a staff responsive to the needs of each child as a unique learner who has the right to self-determination.

Shared Ownership: The Environment

Shared ownership (Zhao, 2018b) is one of the most prominent changes Ritchie has institutionalized at Annesley. The young children at the school are engaged in all aspects of the school as co-owners rather than as passive recipients of instructions. They are leading, in partnership with the school's leadership and an outside consultant, the re-creation of the school's Child Safe Policy. They are planning and leading every aspect of the school's major events. They are developing a brand-new student leadership structure. They are involved in the hiring of new staff by generating key questions and conducting interviews with short-listed candidates. They are, in essence, exercising self-determination over the operation of their school.

Shared ownership means adults and children in a school are co-owners of the school and what happens in the school. Shared ownership ensures that students have control over their educational experiences. It is a necessary condition that enables students to both contribute to and take responsibility for the culture, infrastructure, and resources in their school. Without shared ownership, there is very little that students can take charge of or practice self-determination over. Moreover, shared ownership helps students think beyond their own interests to consider the interests of others and the community as a whole, because shared ownership means shared responsibility. Students, when granted the right to take control, to exercise self-determination, are simultaneously expected to accept the responsibility of their actions and decisions. Not only are they expected to live with the consequences themselves but also with others and the school.

Shared ownership, as a form of broad-based ownership, has gained growing interest outside education, particularly in community and business development. It has been proposed as an effective strategy to build more healthy and equitable communities, more successful business development, and effective job creation (Blasi, Freeman, & Kruse, 2014; Kelly, Dubb, & Duncan, 2016). Research suggests that broad-based ownership leads to healthier and more balanced growth and development as well as more equity, as exemplified by the reported benefits of employee-owned businesses and community-owned institutions such as banks and grocery stores (Alperovitz, 2005; Blasi et al., 2014; Kelly et al., 2016).

Shared ownership goes beyond the concept of shared governance, which has been promoted as an organizational model that involves employees in key decision making across many different industries, such as nursing and higher education (Birnbaum, 2004; De Roo, 2017;

Leighninger, 2006; Potter, 2017). It also goes further than the concept of distributed leadership that has gained popularity in leadership studies of schools and other types of organizations (Hairon & Goh, 2015; Harris, 2013; Harris, Leithwood, Day, Sammons, & Hopkins, 2007; Spillane, 2012; Spillane, Halverson, & Diamond, 2001; Tian, Risku, & Collin, 2016). While both shared governance and distributed leadership are concerned about the employees of the organization and possibly other stakeholders, they rarely involve their clients or customers—or students in the case of education institutions—as an integral part of the governance or leadership.

Shared ownership has been proposed and practiced to some extent in education, without using the exact phrase. For example, some form of shared ownership has existed in the long tradition of democratic education and democratic schools (Apple & Beane, 1995; Chamberlin, 2016; Dewey, 1975; Waghid, 2014). The Independent Project at Monument High, discussed in Chapter 1, is another example (Chen, 2014).

However, by and large, shared ownership has rarely been practiced in mainstream educational institutions. Schools have been traditionally owned and thus governed by adults. The majority of schools in the world today treat students as customers or recipients of their services. Students in most schools have little say over the most important elements of the institution where they spend the majority of their time and are the very reason for their existence. The curriculum is owned and controlled by adults, as are the facilities, the rules, the activities and events, and other resources. In other words, students have virtually nothing that is left for them to determine.

Domains for Shared Ownership: Social, Intellectual, and Physical

To create the conditions for student ownership and self-determined learning, students should have shared ownership over all aspects of schooling. That is, students are actively and legitimately engaged in making key decisions about everything that impacts their experiences in the school. The primary domains of schooling that have a direct impact on student learning include social, intellectual, and physical.

The social domain. The social domain of schooling is related to the "soft" environment, or culture, of the school. The social aspects of schooling, as part of the so-called hidden curriculum (Wren, 1999), have a significant impact on students' education experiences. An important factor affecting the culture of a school has to do with how students are viewed in relation to adults. Are they viewed, like the adults, as equal members of the school community? Are they considered to have the right to self-determination? Are they viewed as having the capability to exercise their self-determination? Are they viewed as having the ability and willingness to contribute to the good of the community?

Admittedly, children, particularly younger children, are not as cognitively and socially-emotionally mature as adults, nor do they have the same level of expertise, and there is a lot they need to learn and experience in order to become fully functional members of a society. Regardless, they should be treated as equal members of a community with the full right to self-determination. They should be able to participate in decisions over and give consent to actions that affect their well-being. Moreover, it is through experiences as fully participating members that children develop the capacity for performing civic duties as self-determining citizens. Finally, experiences of democratic schools have shown that children can indeed participate responsibly and competently as equal members of school communities (Zhao, 2012).

Viewing students as equals to adults in a school is a necessary mindset for creating a culture that enables self-determined learning. Also necessary are mechanisms that ensure students can participate in making decisions that impact their welfare. Such mechanisms can take different forms. A frequently used mechanism in democratic schools is the regular school meetings open to all students and staff and sometimes parents. These meetings are the primary venue for making decisions about school matters that range from creating rules and regulations, settling conflicts, and examining and approving expenditures to appointing or dismissing staff, deciding the structure of the school day, and purchasing equipment or books. Other mechanisms include committees dedicated to particular issues, such as developing safety policies or handling personnel matters.

Whatever the format, the key is to have institutionalized opportunities for students to have a genuine voice in decisions that matter to their experiences in the school. Students should be actively involved in making and enforcing rules that govern the conduct of members of the entire school community. Furthermore, students should play a significant role in strategic planning, mission development, and major events that have an impact on school culture.

The intellectual domain. The intellectual domain of schooling provides students with the opportunity for cognitive development and knowledge acquisition. The intellectual domain is concerned primarily with the overt curriculum—what courses are offered and who teaches them. To facilitate student ownership and self-determined learning, students should have the right to craft their own education experiences, guided by their strengths and passions, but their choices of courses and other learning activities are confined to what is offered in the school. As a result, what is offered in a school is a community asset that affects everyone in the community. Shared ownership thus should include ownership of the courses and other curricular activities in the school. In this arrangement, students have equal rights to and bear the same responsibility for increasing the quality and quantity of curricular offerings in schools.

Shared ownership of the intellectual domain is ensured through institutionalized mechanisms. Again, like mechanisms for shared ownership of the social domain of schooling, mechanisms for supporting shared ownership of the intellectual domain take many forms. For example, at the Sudbury School, a pioneer in democratic education, students and staff together decide what courses are offered each year (Greenberg et al., 2005; Zhao, 2012). Templestowe College, an innovative government school in Australia, includes students in curriculum committees (Zhao, 2018b). Curriculum committees or subcommittees are bodies that make decisions about curriculum matters: what courses are offered, when, by whom, and so on. They also review the current offerings and survey students regarding courses that need to be removed, added, or improved.

The physical domain. The physical domain of schooling is the physical environment and facilities, such as the library and meeting places. The physical domain also includes school grounds, computing equipment, lab equipment, and other physical resources. The physical aspects of schools are important community assets that affect everyone. Students sharing the ownership of a school's physical domain is a necessary condition for enabling student ownership and self-determined learning. In other words, students should have the rights to and responsibilities for the improvement, management, maintenance, and uses of the physical environment, facilities, and equipment of a school.

There are many different mechanisms to ensure shared ownership of the physical domain. At Templestowe College, for example, students own the library, as the school does not have an adult librarian in the space. But they have rules and are encouraged to bring books from home. At Annesley, the students were part of the design team that developed the new outdoor playground. They are also the owners of a coffee shop.

Classrooms

Shared ownership should not exist only at the school level. It should be practiced at the course level as well. For example, Beijing Academy, a new innovative secondary school in Beijing, China, changed the ownership of field trips into shared ownership. The school makes extended culture study trips to distant places an important component of its curriculum. Previously, the adults owned these trips: they planned where to go, how to get there, where to stay, and what to do. They bore all the responsibilities for all issues related to the trip: budgeting, safety, and content. Now the school asks the students to develop and defend their proposed trips before a committee of adults and students. Students and adults thus share the ownership and, as a result, responsibilities.

Forms of Shared Ownership:
Representative and Direct Democracy

To enable shared ownership, schools need to develop institutional infrastructures for shared governance. The concept of shared ownership should be explicitly codified in school constitutions or bylaws. The shared ownership code should clearly describe how students can participate in the governance of the school and in what areas they can participate.

Schools can decide, collectively, how students can participate in shared governance: through direct or representative participation. Direct participation, like direct democracy, means that all students and adults are entitled to participate in making decisions through directly voicing their opinions, such as voting. Representative participation, like representative democracy, means a small number of students and adults directly participate in making decisions. The decision makers are elected as representatives of their respective constituents. Election or full participation of all students is key to genuine shared ownership. It is a significant distinction from the common practice of having adults appoint a few students for positions on leadership teams.

It may be impractical or inefficient for all students to directly participate in making all decisions, especially in large schools. Representative participation may work better than direct participation in most cases, where instead of involving all students in all decisions, schools can establish committees with representatives elected by students. With today's technology, schools can consult students and parents directly through social media or websites. Students can directly vote on large issues as well.

Shared ownership, as a necessary condition to enable self-determined learning, takes time, effort, and resources. Thus, schools must have protected time for students and staff to exercise their shared ownership. For example, schools should have dedicated days and times for elections or other forms of venues through which the entire community can participate in major decision making. Schools should also develop mechanisms through which students and staff can have their voices heard on a regular basis. Additionally, schools should also create opportunities for students and staff to learn about shared ownership and help them learn about democracy and citizenship through authentic experiences.

Implementing Shared Ownership: Evolutionary Revolution

For schools that do not have a tradition of democratic education, which are in the majority, implementing shared ownership is no easy task. It is similar to the transformation of an authoritarian society into a true democracy. And that can take tremendous effort and a long time. While quite often the transformation of political systems may begin with a revolution, sometimes violent and bloody, the transformation in schools should not and cannot be that abrupt and violent. Instead, revolutions in education have to be evolutionary for many reasons that have been well documented by scholars (Tyack & Cuban, 1995; Tyack & Tobin, 1994). The persistence of traditional practices, the organizational inertia, the doubts about the proposed changes, and the concerns about the potential negative outcomes are just some of the factors standing to resist and quash any efforts at revolutionary changes.

There are a number of strategies to start the evolutionary revolution of implementing shared ownership in schools. The first is *from peripheral to core*. That is, changes should start from the peripheral practices of a school and gradually move toward the core. It is best to start making changes to things that most people do not care about or are not even aware of because such changes are less likely to be resisted or rejected. For example, making changes to extracurricular activities is much less likely to meet with resistance than changing the core curriculum. Similarly, making changes to elective courses is less likely to attract resistance than touching the core curriculum. As a result, implementing shared ownership in extracurricular activities and elective courses is much easier than forcing teachers to share ownership with students in core courses. Likewise, having students share ownership in art and music classes can be much easier than in math and science.

Following this strategy, a school can begin implementing shared ownership in a number of ways. First, it could have students and adults share the ownership of extracurricular activities. A committee on extracurricular activities can be formed with representatives of students and staff to design, develop, and implement extracurricular activities and govern the development and distribution of resources needed for such activities.

Since many extracurricular activities already have a strong flavor of student governance, this should be the easiest to start with. Second, schools could consider implementing shared ownership in a small percentage of courses. For example, a school could dedicate one day a week to activities co-owned by staff and students. Similarly, schools can choose to dedicate a certain number of hours of each school day or a number of weeks each term for this purpose. Third, a school could consider implementing shared ownership over certain areas of its physical environment, such as the library, the media center, or vegetable gardens.

The second strategy is *invitation instead of imposition*. Education leaders interested in a new initiative quite often instinctually think about implementing it in the entire school or system. This is admirable but often unrealistic. A more productive strategy is to issue the invitation of change to everyone but never impose it on anyone. Attempting to implement an initiative that affects everyone is a sure way to invite resistance and rejection because not everyone is open to or interested in making changes. More important, most people instinctively reject impositions because of their own desire for self-determination. However, an invitation to participate in implementing a new initiative simply presents an opportunity for those who are willing or even eager to change. In most schools, there are always a small number of teachers, leaders, and students who are unhappy with the current practices and are searching for opportunities to make changes.

Following this strategy, a school can implement shared ownership for the willing—the willing students, the willing teachers, and the willing parents. It is like incubating a new school within the existing school. The new school, completely co-owned by staff and students, invites students and teachers who are interested in the new paradigm of education, but it is not forced upon all students. This model may be especially powerful to students and teachers who are dissatisfied with and are not served well by existing practices.

Personalized Learning Plans: The Learning

Aside from opportunities for self-determining action over their learning environment through shared ownership, students should be able to exercise control over their own learning. In other words, students should be able to determine the outcomes and pathways to achieve the outcomes of their own learning. The outcomes and pathways include both short-term ones that span over a term or a year and long-term ones that span their entire school career.

Students exerting self-determination over their learning can only happen under a number of conditions, including a reconceptualization of both the outcomes and pathways of learning. As practiced in the majority of schools today, all students are expected to achieve a uniform set of outcomes following a uniform pathway. The uniform set of outcomes are often prescribed by government authorities, codified in curriculum standards, and enforced through standardized high-stakes tests. They can also be set by other institutions that have decisive power over a student's future opportunities. An example is the College Board in the United States, which offers the exams that can affect a student's chance for admission to colleges. The underlying assumption of a uniform set of outcomes is the belief that all students need the same set of knowledge, skills, and abilities to succeed in the world.

Not only are students expected to achieve the same outcomes but also they are expected to follow a uniform pathway to reach their goals. Students are often grouped by their biological age and expected to take the same courses as peers their age. Curriculum standards typically expect students of the same age to master the same knowledge and skills. Assessments are often conducted each year to ensure that students are progressing similarly and as expected. The underlying assumption of a uniform pathway is that all children have similar talents, passions, and opportunities to progress at a similar speed.

It goes without saying that when the outcomes and pathways are predetermined, students have little room to exercise self-determination over what they want to learn and how they want to learn. But this arrangement is neither desirable nor necessary. As Yong Zhao argues in his book *Reach for Greatness: Personalizable Education for All Children* (Zhao, 2018b), it is impossible for all students to achieve the same outcomes at a similar pace because they have different talents, different interests, and more important, different opportunities and access to resources. Moreover, Zhao points out that the belief that all students need the same set of skills and knowledge for success is rendered obsolete by recent technological changes. Instead of a homogenous set of skills and knowledge, a unique jagged profile of skills and knowledge that makes each and every student uniquely great is more desirable for success in the future (Zhao, 2018a).

Unique greatness means that students build on their unique strengths, passions, and contexts to develop a unique set of knowledge and skills. Each student has a unique combination of abilities that sets her apart from others. As such, students should not be expected to pursue a uniform set of learning outcomes. Instead, students pursue their individual learning goals. This does not mean common skills and knowledge are not required of all students, because to perform civic duties and function as members of a common society requires some basic knowledge and skills, as well as values shared by all.

Individual outcomes can only be achieved through individual pathways. That is, each student constructs and follows his highly personalized learning plan. Moreover, given the vast diversity in talents, interests, opportunities, and access to resources, learning pathways must be personalized to meet the needs of each and every student. This means students need to have control over their learning process.

The new conceptualization of learning outcomes and pathways creates —in fact, demands—self-determination. That is, students must be the owners of their learning enterprise. They must decide what to learn and how to learn, with the help of adults.

One way for adults to help is through the creation and execution of a personalized learning plan (PLP). A PLP (or whatever name we use) is documentation of learning goals and pathways to achieve the goals for each student. This documentation should be created primarily by students or at least with significant input from students, in consultation with parents and teachers. It should be dynamic, updated whenever needed.

The content of a PLP may vary, but there are a few essential elements that should be included. First, it should include students' descriptions of their unique strengths and interests. Second, it should include students' articulation of their plans to improve their strengths and pursue their interests. Third, it should document students' justification of how the unique strengths and interests can be used to create value for others and the broader society. Fourth, it should include students' proposals for ways to assess and evidence of their progress. Fifth, it should include adults' reactions to students' input.

The process of creating a PLP is as important as the documentation itself. The process should be a dialogue between the students and adults, through which students learn about their strengths and passions, and more important, the meaning of self-determination—its potentials and boundaries and its inherent freedom and accountability. A PLP is a living document, and thus the process never stops and is iterative. While they should be reviewed at the beginning and end of each academic year, if not more frequently, students, parents, or teachers can propose to review them at any time during the year.

A PLP is in some ways similar to the Individualized Education Program (IEP) required for students with disabilities in the United States (Individuals with Disabilities Education Act, 2004), particularly in terms of how they are created. But there are a number of fundamental conceptual differences between them. First, a PLP applies to all students, while an IEP only applies to students with disabilities. In our view, every student has strengths and weaknesses, or areas of ability and limitations. Thus every student deserves to have her education individualized.

Second, an IEP is deficit-driven. It is to help students who are not as strong as others in some domains to catch up with their peers or to become "normal." A PLP focuses on students' strengths and interests. The "deficiency" or "gap" of knowledge and skills in a PLP is defined as the distance between where the student is and where he wants to go. It is not defined by curriculum standards or statistical norms.

Finally, an IEP decides learning goals for all students according to the same set of predetermined outcomes in curriculum standards and thus limits the definition of learning to a very narrow spectrum of subjects. A PLP follows the student's passions and interests. If a student is interested in something that's not offered in the school at the moment, the school could (and should) find ways to provide such opportunity or at least permit the student to learn on his own from other sources, such as online. In other words, a PLP is not prescriptive. It is descriptive.

The Flexibility Mindset: Organization

To enable student ownership and self-determined learning—to share ownership with students and to support personalized learning plans for all students—requires flexibility. Schools cannot be run as a well-managed factory that follows the same routine each and every day. Instead, they are dynamic communities of living, maturing, and learning human beings that are responsive to constant changes. They do not exist to enforce standards but to meet the needs of children. Thus, schools should have maximum flexibility to be able to respond to new opportunities, emerging needs, and unexpected problems.

Flexibility applies to all aspects of a school and all members of the school community. That is, everyone should have a flexibility mindset. A flexibility mindset sees value in changes. People with a flexibility mindset also believe that plans, no matter how carefully thought out, would always require change because of unexpected disruptions or outcomes.

A flexibility mindset is required to support the effective execution of a PLP. It happens often that a student discovers that a course does not meet her needs as expected when developing the PLP. Instead of following the original plan, she is better served by dropping a course and taking another one, negotiating with the teacher for different content, or working on something else entirely with the consent of involved adult stakeholders.

Similarly, students may discover that they do not have the resources or skills to complete a school project as planned. Instead of seeing it as a failure, teachers with a flexibility mindset would consider it an excellent learning opportunity. Depending on the contextual specifics of the project, the teacher could suggest to students that they take more time to acquire the needed resources or skills or abandon the project. It is also possible that some students discover new interests and opportunities that are worthier of pursuing while doing a project or taking a course. People with a flexibilty mindset might consider abandoning the old course or project in order to pursue the newly discovered interest.

To foster and grow the flexibility mindset, schools need a culture that embraces change as a valuable learning experience. Adjustments are not a waste of time or resources but necessary. Changes are normal and expected. After all, learning is about change; it is about discovering passions and strengths.

Schools can build intuitional infrastructure to support the flexibility mindset. Courses do not need to be all the same duration. Some can be for one week, some for two weeks, and others for 10 weeks. Physical facilities need to be flexible as well. Not all rooms need to be the same size. Not all desks need to be arranged the same way. Not all technology should be the same kind. Not all courses have to be taught by staff; students or community members can teach some courses.

Self-determined learning is driven by students. Thus, traditional ways of organizing students need to be abolished to enable self-determined learning. First, students no longer need to be organized into grade levels according to biological age. Students from different ages can organize themselves into different learning teams (e.g., the Independent Project included students from different grade levels).

Flexibility is also required in organizing students into classes. Self-determined learning needs the support and guidance of adults, but adults should not be the center around which students are organized. Students cannot be forced into same-sized class groups. Some groups may be large and others may be very small. It all depends on the interest of students.

Reconceptualized Teaching: The Teachers

Another key enabling condition for self-determined learning is reconceptualized teaching and teachers. To support self-determined learning, teaching needs to shift from transmitting knowledge and skills to supporting the growth of students as human beings. Teaching, rather than focusing on fixing students' deficits as measured by testing or standards, needs to focus on what students can and want to do. It needs to help each and every student identify and enhance his unique strengths and passions. Furthermore, teaching should strive to develop social-emotional qualities, nurture creativity, and foster the capacity for self-determination. In practice, teaching in support of self-determined learning starts with the unique passion and talents of each child rather than curriculum standards or textbooks. Teaching is to create opportunities for individual students. Its aim is to help each child to become the master of their learning.

This new conceptualization of teaching is made possible by recent technological advances and is supported by new discoveries about the nature of learners and learning. Children today have ready and easy access to a vast range of learning opportunities beyond their teachers through technology. Children are capable of becoming self-organizing learners (Mitra, 2007, 2012), and they learn best when engaged in relevant, authentic, and challenging experiences. As a result, teachers no longer need to teach in the traditional sense—that is, serve as the sole source of knowledge and the only organizer of learning. In other words, teachers no longer need to perform the traditional repetitive and mechanical instructional duties (Zhao, Zhang, Lei, & Qiu, 2015). As a result, they have more flexibility to organize their classes and work with individual students. Moreover, they can delegate the instructional activities that focus on knowledge transmission and cognitive skills development to technology, so they can focus more on the human aspects of education.

In self-determined education, teachers' roles differ from those traditionally conceived. Teachers are no longer instructors; they are *life coaches*. They work with students to identify, develop, and achieve personal learning goals. They guide students to learn about their strengths and weaknesses, explore possibilities, develop high aspirations, and try out their ambitions. They provide students with challenges and encourage students. They help students manage and learn from failures and successes. They are concerned about students' social, emotional, and psychological well-being in addition to their academic performance.

Teachers also assume the role of curators of learning opportunities and resources. Instead of being the source of knowledge, they critically examine, thoughtfully select, and carefully construct a "museum" of learning opportunities for students. The opportunities and resources are curated in response to the needs of individual students. Furthermore, teachers co-design learning pathways with individual students and help students learn to discover and manage their own learning opportunities and resources.

To enable self-determined education, teachers work collaboratively as a community. Teachers in a school have complementary talents, expertise, and passions. They are not merely replaceable mechanical instructional machines but unique human educators with different profiles of expertise and talents. Thus, instead of teaching a group of students in isolated classrooms, teachers work with individual students as consultants in their areas of expertise and passion.

In self-determined education, teachers assume the roles of community organizers and project leaders. Self-determined learning does not mean students always learn alone. Rather, they learn through authentic projects in collaboration with others. Meaningful and significant projects necessarily require the participation and contribution of many individuals with different and complementary talents and interests. Students learn in communities. Teachers are responsible for supporting the development of these communities, facilitating the development of rules that make these communities operate effectively, and ensuring these communities are beneficial to all members.

Self-Determined Education

Self-determined education is a radical departure from conventional education. To fully and truly give the right to self-determination to children requires radical changes to how educational institutions have traditionally operated. We need to rethink what it means to be educated and how education is delivered, because self-determined education requires a different set of conditions from conventional education.

This chapter proposes some of the enabling conditions for self-determined education that are summarized in the Research to Practice section that closes the chapter. These new conditions are very difficult to create in traditional schools, which are constrained by a system that has evolved for more than a century. The conditions suggested in this chapter are ideal targets we should aim for rather than immediate requirements. But we should get started right now.

Research to Practice: Enabling Student Ownership and Self-Determined Learning

Shared ownership means adults and children in a school are co-owners of the school and what happens in the school and ensures that students have control over their educational experiences.

Shared ownership goes beyond simply shared governance. Students should be actively and legitimately engaged in making key decisions about everything that impacts their experiences in the school. The primary domains of schooling that have a direct impact on student learning include social, intellectual, and physical.

The *social domain* of schooling is related to the "soft" environment, or culture, of the school.

- An important factor affecting the culture of a school has to do with how students are viewed in relation to adults. Children, particularly younger children, are not as cognitively and socially-emotionally mature as adults, nor do they have the same level of expertise. Regardless, they should be able to participate in decisions over and give consent to actions that affect their well-being.
- It is through experiences as fully participating members that children develop the capacity for performing civic duties as self-determining citizens.
- Students should be actively involved in making and enforcing rules that govern the conduct of members of the entire school community.
- Students should play a significant role in strategic planning, mission development, and major events that have an impact on school culture.

The *intellectual domain* of schooling concerns primarily the overt curriculum—what courses are offered and who teaches them.

- Students should have the right to craft their own education experiences, guided by their strengths and passions.
- Shared ownership should include ownership of the courses and other curricular activities in the school. In this arrangement, students have equal rights to and bear the same responsibility for increasing the quality and quantity of curricular offerings in schools.

The *physical domain* of schooling is the physical environment and facilities, such as the library, meeting places, school grounds, computing equipment, lab equipment, and other physical resources.

To enable shared ownership, schools need to develop institutional infrastructures for shared governance. The concept of shared ownership should be explicitly codified in school constitutions or bylaws. Schools can decide, collectively, how students can participate in shared governance—through direct participation or representative participation.

- *Direct participation* means that all students and adults are entitled to participate in making decisions through directly voicing their opinions, such as voting.
- *Representative participation* means a small number of students and adults directly participate in making decisions. The decision makers are elected as representatives of their respective constituents.

Shared ownership takes time, effort, and resources.

- Schools must have protected time for students and staff to exercise their shared ownership.
- Schools should create opportunities for students and staff to learn about shared ownership and help them learn about democracy and citizenship through authentic experiences.

There are a number of strategies to implement shared ownership in schools.

- The first strategy is *from peripheral to core*. Changes start from peripheral practices of a school and gradually move toward the core.
- The second strategy is *invitation instead of imposition*. A school can implement shared ownership for the willing—the willing students, the willing teachers, and the willing parents.

Students should be able to exercise control over their own learning. When the outcomes and pathways are predetermined, students have little room to exercise self-determination over what they want to learn and how they want to learn. Individual outcomes can only be achieved through individual pathways.

- One way for adults to help is through the creation and execution of a personalized learning plan (PLP).
- This documentation should be created primarily by students or at least with significant input from students, in consultation with parents and teachers.
- Although the content of a PLP may vary, a few essential elements that should be included are:
  - Students' descriptions of their unique strengths and interests.
  - Students' articulation of their plans to improve their strengths and pursue their interests.
  - Students' justification of how the unique strengths and interests can be used to create value for others and the broader society.
  - Students' proposals for ways and evidence to assess their progress.
  - Adults' reactions to students' input.

Schools should have maximum flexibility to be able to respond to new opportunities, emerging needs, and unexpected problems. To foster and grow the flexibility mindset, schools need a culture that embraces change as a valuable learning experience.

Another key enabling condition for self-determined learning is reconceptualized teaching and teachers:

- Instead of transmitting uniformly prescribed knowledge and skills to all students, teaching needs to focus on supporting the growth of students as human beings.
- Instead of focusing on fixing students' deficits as measured by testing or standards, teaching should focus on identifying and enhancing individual strengths and passions.
- Instead of transmitting knowledge and skills in specific subjects, teaching should strive to develop social-emotional qualities, nurture creativity, and foster the capacity for self-determination.

continued

Research to Practice: Enabling Student Ownership and Self-Determined Learning (*continued*)

In self-determined education

- *Teaching starts with the children's passion and talent.* Teaching is not to instruct but to create opportunities for individual students, to help individual students pursue their interests and enhance their abilities, and to help students identify and access resources from within and outside the school.
- *Teachers become masterful life coaches* who help students identify, develop, and achieve personal goals, learn about their strengths and weaknesses, explore possibilities, develop high aspirations, and try out their ambitions.
- *Teachers work collaboratively as a community.* They do not teach a group of students in isolated classrooms but work with individual students as consultants in their areas of expertise and passion.
- *Teachers are community organizers and project leaders.* Self-determined learning does not mean students always learn alone. Instead very often students learn through authentic projects in collaboration with others.

Teaching Strategies for Student Ownership and Self-Determined Learning

Teachers at Crozet Elementary School in Albemarle County, Virginia, prioritize enhancing their students' beliefs about themselves as self-determined learners. Crozet principal, Gwedette Crummie, says that their goal is "to teach students to be self-determined . . . it's teaching them that they can do anything" (Schmitz, 2016). All 5th grade students at Crozet begin the year with a focus on their hopes and dreams—their passions and interests—and use these to set goals for their futures (Schmitz, 2016).

In Chapter 3, we presented a framework to guide the design of interventions and strategies to promote self-determined learning. We now turn to the strategies that emerge from the framework that teachers can implement to promote student ownership and self-determined learning. The Research and Theory section that follows provides a reminder of the structure of Causal Agency Theory, which forms part of that framework.

Research and Theory: Causal Agency Theory

A *causal agent* is someone who makes or causes things to happen (self-determinism versus other-determinism) in their own life.

Causal Agency Theory views self-determined action as being energized by the basic psychological needs for autonomy, competence, and relatedness, as described by SDT. Motivations energize action. Efforts to act autonomously (volitionally) and fulfill basic psychological needs result in a causal action sequence. That causal action sequence consists of

- *Volitional actions.* The self-initiation of actions that enable one to set and pursue goals associated with one's preferences, interests, and passions.
- *Agentic actions.* Self-regulated and self-directed actions that enable one to progress toward freely chosen goals.
- *Action-control beliefs.* Beliefs that enable one to act with a sense of personal empowerment as an agent in one's learning and to take ownership over learning (Shogren, Wehmeyer, & Palmer, 2017).

Repeated experiences with this causal action sequence result in perceptions of oneself as a causal agent and, over time, in the development of self-determination.

Engaging students in opportunities to learn, practice, and implement skills pertaining to volitional and agentic action (discussed next), combined with the general principles of student ownership and self-determined learning related to autonomy, competence, and relatedness supports, leads to the development of action-control beliefs that support students' efforts to act as causal agents. We'll focus in this chapter on strategies to promote volitional and agentic action, and will then provide an overview of a teaching model designed to enable teachers to teach students to self-regulate problem solving to set a goal, create an action plan, and adjust the plan or goal as necessary to achieve the goal.

Teaching Volitional Action

To act volitionally, students must use skills that enable them to initiate and engage in causal action. As shown in Figure 5.1, these include problem-solving, decision-making, goal-setting, and planning skills. Before we introduce strategies to teach these skills, it is important to remember that the goal for such instruction should be *engagement in* and not solely *mastery of* these skills and actions. By involving students in setting goals or solving problems, we maximize the potential that they will acquire some elements of these processes, improve their abilities in these areas, and improve their capacity for self-determined learning.

5.1 Component Elements of Volitional Action

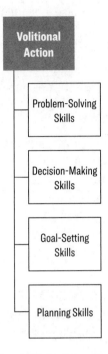

Source: From *The Self-Determined Learning Model of Instruction: Teacher's Guide*, by K. A. Shogren, S. K. Raley, K. M. Burke, and M. L. Wehmeyer, 2019, Lawrence, KS: Kansas University Center on Developmental Disabilities. Copyright 2019 by Kansas University Center on Developmental Disabilities. Adapted with permission.

Teach Your Students to Engage in Solving Problems

Solving problems is essential if students are to engage in self-determined learning. If you already know something, you don't need to learn it. If you don't know something, that is, by definition, a problem! Ronald Beghetto (2018), editor of the *Journal of Creative Behavior*, said: "a problem is not a problem unless it involves some level of uncertainty" (p. 3). Creativity, entrepreneurship, critical thinking . . . all rely on tackling and working to address uncertainty; that is, to solve problems.

A problem is quite simply a situation, activity, or task for which a solution or pathway is unknown or unclear. Posing problems for students to solve in the form of questions for inquiry is at the heart of what we do in education. "What are the mechanisms and factors that promote plant growth?" "How does climate change impact food distribution worldwide?" "What did Hamlet mean when he said, 'The play is the thing'?" These are the types of problems we pose to students every day to stimulate learning.

We're talking here about problems in the broader sense of learning challenges, as Beghetto frames them, and not the narrower sense of solving arithmetic equations. We're also not intending to pack the meaning of the word problem with the negative connotations that many people associate with "having a problem." Many "problems" are social in nature in that they involve interactions with teachers, peers, experts, and others. Thus, solving problems is important not only in the sense of addressing a learning challenge but also in interacting with others to be able to do so more autonomously.

Based on the problem-solving research and steps identified in the Research and Theory section that follows, the first step in teaching problem solving is to teach a positive problem orientation, which refers to a student's beliefs and orientation toward the problem-solving task. D'Zurilla, Nezu, and Maydeu-Olivares (2004) refer to such an orientation as a general quality or tendency to

- Appraise a problem as a "challenge" (i.e., opportunity for benefit or gain);
- Believe that problems are solvable;
- Believe in one's personal ability to solve problems successfully;
- Believe that successful problem solving takes time and effort; and
- Commit oneself to solving problems with dispatch rather than avoiding them." (p. 15)

Research and Theory: Development of and Steps to Problem Solving

Children generally develop problem-solving abilities in late elementary and early middle/junior high school, but providing opportunities to participate in the problem-solving process is important from early childhood on. The problem-solving model that has driven most research and intervention efforts in education and other applied disciplines is that of Thomas D'Zurilla and colleagues. In *Social Problem Solving: Theory, Research, and Training,* these researchers detailed a five-step training model to teach problem solving:

1. Problem orientation;
2. Problem definition and formulation;
3. Generation of alternative solutions;
4. Decision making; and
5. Solution implementation. (D'Zurilla et al., 2004, pp. 14–15)

When people are autonomously motivated, as we discussed in Chapter 2, they tend to show more persistence at completing problem-solving tasks (Shogren & Wehmeyer, 2017). Thus, educators can support students to approach problem solving with a positive orientation by implementing the autonomy, competency, and relatedness supports discussed.

Next, students need to learn to more precisely define their problem by gathering information about the problem; generating possible solutions to the problem; weighing the pros and cons associated with solutions to make a decision about what is potentially the best solution to the problem; and implementing that solution. Beghetto (2018) simplified this basic process into four "action principles" associated with teaching students to address challenges: Stop, Think, Do, and Learn (p. 26). Each of these action principles has two sub-actions.

Stop. Stopping to (1) explore and (2) prepare needs to happen first so that students can gather information about the problem, refine their understanding of the problem, and generate possible solutions. Repeated experiences with solving problems make this process almost automatic to adults, but when first learning to solve problems, this step can be more difficult than presumed. Nezu and D'Zurilla (1981) identified the problem-definition and formulation stage as

- Gathering facts;
- Distinguishing among facts, opinions, and inferences;
- Discarding irrelevant information;
- Identifying desired outcomes for the problem-solution process; and
- Identifying factors and circumstances that might be barriers to the solution. (p. 101)

Students tend to make more global attributions to problems, even into adolescence. That means they are not yet as skilled at narrowing down the problem to one that can be solved. Sometimes it is a matter of identifying which aspect of a problem to begin to solve; other times it involves refining a problem to one that is solvable. Big problems—like increasing the adoption of renewable energy—have many parts, and narrowing down possible problems to solve within that broader problem involves research, investigation, and exploration.

On the other hand, sometimes the "problem" immediately perceived is not even the right problem, and one has to drill down to get to the real problem. In *How Not to Be Wrong* (2014), author Jordan Ellenberg tells the story of a military group that was charged with solving the problem of how best to protect aircraft being fired upon by Nazi anti-aircraft guns during World War II air raids. The initial analysis of the problem concentrated on examining the distribution of bullet holes in the body of fighter airplanes that returned from missions. These analyses determined that the fuselage, fuel systems, and underbody of the planes had the highest density of bullet holes per square foot. The solution proposed by the problem analysis was to put more armor where the highest distribution of bullet holes existed. The problem that solution created was that by adding armor across these areas of each plane, they became heavier, which reduced their fuel efficiency, in turn limiting the range on which missions could be flown. Finally, one of the team members suggested that they were working on the wrong problem. The relevant problem was the bullet distribution in planes that *did not* return from combat missions. The team managed to retrieve several planes that had been shot down and, sure enough, the highest density of bullet holes in these was in the engine. The armor needed to go there, and not elsewhere, which also reduced the weight of adding armor. Wrong problem, wrong solution!

Think. Beghetto's second action principal is to teach children to think (1) divergently and (2) convergently. Thinking divergently means looking at problems or challenges in new and different ways and coming up with original solutions. Thinking convergently means evaluating from among possible solutions that have been generated. This takes time and practice, and even older youth need to be supported to use divergent and convergent thinking to generate and evaluate options. As previously stated, being an autonomy-supportive teacher involves providing supportive responses that enable students to think on their own rather than just answering questions for them. Beghetto notes that teachers can provide feedback that encourages the student to "put a new twist on that idea to make it your own" (p. 31).

Do. During the *Think* action step, students generate possible solutions to the problem that they then refine during the *Stop* action step. In the *Do* action step, students (1) plan and (2) test as they try out the solutions that seem to have promise. We need to teach students to plan out steps to implementing the most promising solutions, to ask what is and what is not working and, if the latter, whether it is the solution itself or the implementation that might be the barrier.

Learn. Children become more effective problem solvers by solving problems, reflecting on the processes and what worked (or not), and identifying and revising their processes for the future. We can help students find the optimal fit between what they know and the problems they tackle, particularly when they are first learning to solve problems. And, there are real-world problems that children and youth face, the solutions to which matter more to them than abstract problems. Think about why Alice Macmillan was so passionate about solving the problem of epilepsy awareness we talked about in Chapter 3. And creating learning communities in which students feel safe is important if students are to learn problem-solving skills, for the simple reason that we all learn to solve problems by trying and getting it wrong, trying again, and so on.

There are other models with which to teach problem solving. Cynthia Benjamin (1996) developed and evaluated a program to get students thinking about problems they encounter at school that followed a four-step process:

1. Understand
2. Plan and Solve
3. Check
4. Review

Stephen Krulik and Jesse Rudnick (1995) forwarded a five-step process:

1. Read and Think
2. Explore and Plan
3. Select a Strategy
4. Find an Answer
5. Reflect and Extend

But you can easily see that these follow processes similar to Beghetto's action principles and the sequence laid out by D'Zurilla and colleagues. These are the steps you use every day. Often it is as simple as involving your students in your own problem-solving process!

Teach creativity. Let's talk a moment about an element of problem solving and decision making, as well as one of the most visible elements of most 21st century learning taxonomies: creativity. Generating alternatives in both the problem-solving and decision-making processes involves creativity skills. All children are born with "the ability to come up with new ideas, methods, theories, concepts, and products" (Zhao, 2018, p. 38). It is the responsibility of the educator to provide opportunities for students to exercise their creative muscles and learn strategies that enable them to build those muscles.

As psychologist Robert Sternberg and colleagues pointed out, the capacity to be creative "is not only what enables us to come up with new ideas (whatever the field); it is also the skill that enables us to deal with new situations or problems that we have never confronted before" (Sternberg, Jarvin, & Grigorenko, 2009, p. 35). Teaching students to solve problems and make decisions teaches them to be creative. Tasks that explicitly state that students *brainstorm* or *create* or *invent* or *imagine* or *explore* are opportunities for students to learn to be creative.

Moreover, it is important to encourage students to learn to generate many ideas (fluency), as well as to generate original ideas. The former (fluency) requires that you "encourage quantity, not quality (defer judgment)" and "push for more ideas" (Sternberg et al., 2009, p. 37). An exercise to promote originality is to have the class generate a list of the "usual ideas" that might be solutions to a problem, and then have each student think of at least one idea that is not on that list (Sternberg et al., 2009). Again, it's important to encourage originality and not whether something is right or wrong. The purpose of generating ideas is…, well, to generate ideas!

Teach Your Students to Engage in Making Decisions

A decision, put simply, is a choice writ large. We often use the words *choice* and *decision* interchangeably in our daily conversations. A decision, though, is a process that begins by solving a problem (What are the options from which I am to make a decision?); it involves weighing the consequences (pros and cons) of various decision options, taking into account one's preferences, interests, values, and beliefs, and then, ultimately, choosing one of the options. Developmentally, children acquire the requisite skills for decision making in early adolescence, after they have learned how to solve problems.

Decision making is ultimately a goal-oriented enterprise. We have identified eight primary steps in the decision-making process:

1. Recognition of the circumstances that lead to the need for a decision.
2. Awareness of the need to make a decision.
3. Identification of the goal to which the decision is in service.
4. Identification of action alternatives.
5. Determination of the consequences of each action alternative.
6. Determination of the probability of each consequence occurring if action is undertaken.
7. Establishment of the relative importance (value or utility) of each action alternative and consequence.
8. Integration of the probability and importance determination to identify the most attractive course of action. (Wehmeyer & Shogren, 2017, p. 263)

Israeli psychologist Ruth Beyth-Marom has spent her career examining risk taking in adolescents and their decision-making processes. Unlike problem solving, for which there are often right or wrong solutions, decision making involves uncertainty, even when coming to a decision point.

The Research and Theory section that follows provides information from research that influences risk taking and decision making.

Research and Theory: Elements of Risk Taking and Decision Making

Elements of risk taking and decision making that influence decisions include

- *Contextuality.* There are a number of ways context influences decision making. These include the cultural context within which a decision is to be made, and how such decisions are made as a function of a culture's emphasis on individualism versus collectivism. Additionally, whether a decision can be made over a period of time versus having to be made quickly influences the relative stress associated with deciding. Finally, there are high-stakes (medical, financial) and low-stakes (what to pack on a trip) decisions, so the contextual elements of how much the decision matters come into play.
- *Personal experience.* Past experiences with and knowledge about decision alternatives, consequences, risks, and benefits influence adult decision making. This is also true for adolescents, but not at the same level. Adolescents use past experiences and knowledge, but that does not as consistently influence their decisions. Peers and the desire for popularity may outweigh past experience or knowledge when an adolescent makes a decision.
- *Complexity.* It stands to reason that more complex decisions often have multiple, and often multiple unsatisfying, possible solutions. Greater complexity can often make the fact-gathering process seem overwhelming and lead to a sense of futility.
- *Risk taking.* Researchers often group decisions into two types: with risk or without risk. Byrnes (2002) questioned that, noting that there are degrees of risk (i.e., "the chance an action could produce an undesirable outcome") in any decision, but it is the consequences of the undesirable outcome that vary (p. 142). The wrong medical decision may have life-impacting consequences, while packing the wrong item likely won't.
- *Preferences and values.* In making a decision, one's preferences, values, and beliefs influence which option is selected, sometimes overriding what might be the logical option. Weighing pros and cons might suggest that I should not purchase the little red Corvette, since it will get terrible gas mileage and cost more to insure and buy. But sometimes one's preferences and passions play out in choosing the red Corvette!

Beyth-Marom and colleagues (1991) emphasized the importance of talking about uncertainty with students, defining what it means, exploring about different kinds of uncertainty, and examining the relationship between uncertainty and the amount or quality of information. The goal is not to eliminate uncertainty but to teach students to manage it.

One research-based process to teach decision-making skills is the GOFER (*G*oals clarification, *O*ption generation, *F*act finding, consideration of *E*ffects, *R*eview) process (Mann, Harmoni, Power, Beswick, &

Ormand, 1989). The Colorado Education Initiative (CEI), a nonprofit initiative to support innovation in public education, has created a process to teach decision-making skills to youth in grades nine to 12. The steps identified by this initiative are

1. Identify a decision that needs to be made.
2. Brainstorm possible options.
3. Identify the positive and negative outcomes for each option.
4. Select an option to implement.
5. Reflect on the decision that was made. (CEI, n.d.)

Keep in mind, when teaching decision making, that younger adolescents are more likely to seek conformity and be influenced by peers when deciding than older adolescents (Mann, Harmoni, & Power, 1989). Also, the ability to weigh the pros and cons of a variety of options is important, and student capacity to generate alternatives and consider consequences improves with age and experience. We learn to solve problems and make decisions by solving problems and making decisions, so provide multiple opportunities for students to do so.

Teach Your Students to Engage in Goal Setting

For purposes of this chapter, we distinguish between goal-setting skills and skills that enable students to attain a goal once it is set; the latter are part of teaching agentic action, discussed next. Setting a goal regulates our actions: when we set a goal, we're more likely to expend resources to address the goal. Goals motivate us to act. It's why we set goals each New Year's Eve. Presumably, if we do so, we are more likely to act on areas that we've identified as important. Why do up to 80 percent of people not follow up on their New Year's resolutions? Psychologists Kaitlin Woolley and Ayelet Fishbach (2017) found that we tend to set long-term goals without specifying short-term objectives, and when we don't see immediate progress, we lose motivation to pursue the goal. So, perhaps we all need instruction in goal setting!

At its core, self-determined learning is a goal-oriented enterprise. Goal setting is typically in response to opportunities in one's life, challenges that are involved in learning or life circumstances, or as a means to express preferences, interests, and passions. Wehmeyer and Mithaug (2006) identified a number of phases to the goal-setting process, described in the Research and Theory section that follows, each of which can become the focus of instruction.

Research and Theory: Phases in the Goal-Setting Process

Phases in the goal-setting process include

- *Goal generation.* Goal setting begins with a self-analysis and exploration of one's strengths, preferences, and needs with regard to the goal area. Students should identify an area in which they want to set a goal, evaluate what they know about the subject of the goal, and prioritize what goal actions might be appropriate.
- *Goal-discrepancy analysis.* Using information from the initial process of goal generation, students next learn to engage in a goal-discrepancy analysis. This means that students need to learn to consider what they know now about the goal area (current status) and the goal status, or what or what they want to know. Students can ask themselves what they need to do to reduce the gap between what they know and what they want or need to know. The need that students have to identify solutions that reduce the discrepancy between what they know and what they want or need to know is called the goal-discrepancy problem. Therefore, one of the critical elements of the goal-setting process is simply a problem-solving process.
- *Capacity-challenge discrepancy analysis.* Part of the goal-discrepancy analysis process is for students to evaluate their capacity to solve the goal-discrepancy problem and to identify new or existing skills and knowledge they will need to use to solve the goal-discrepancy problem and set the goal. This process leads, in turn, to students actually setting a goal.
- *Discrepancy-reduction plan.* Once the student has set a goal, the next step is to create a plan to reduce the discrepancy between what the student knows (current state) and wants to know (goal state). Students set this discrepancy-reduction plan by making choices and decisions about strategies and methods to reduce the discrepancy, basically creating an action plan. An important element of any plan should be how the student will self-monitor implementation of the plan and track progress toward the goal.

This all sounds complicated but teaching goal setting does not have to be that complex. Fundamentally, there are four steps in teaching goal setting:

1. Identifying and enunciating goals.
2. Developing objectives to meet goals.
3. Identifying actions necessary to achieve goals.
4. Tracking and following progress on goals.

Teaching goal identification and enunciation involves teaching students to state goals in ways that make them achievable, including having clear, measurable outcomes. The action planning process includes the development of objectives and actions to meet the goal. Finally, every student can be involved in tracking and following their own progress toward a goal, thus improving autonomous motivation.

Carolyn Maher, a distinguished professor and director of the Rutgers' Davis Institute for Learning has developed a process for teaching self-directed goal setting and self-monitoring of progress. That process, called the Goal-Oriented Approach to Learning (GOAL) involves four steps:

1. *Goal Setting*. At the start of the year, the teacher sits with the student to set an instructional goal for the grading period. The goal is derived from the student's input, past academic performance, and the objectives for the grading period.

2. *Goal-Attainment Scaling*. Next, the student and teacher develop a scale to evaluate attainment of the goals. Possible outcomes of approaching the goal are identified, ranging from less to more desirable, and the teacher emphasizes what an expected (i.e., positive, acceptable) outcome would be, as well as identifying outcomes that would exceed expectations.

3. *Selection of Instructional Strategies*. At weekly meetings, the student and teacher discuss the student's goal progress and possible need for changes and develop a written instructional plan for the upcoming week.

4. *Evaluation of Goal Attainment*. At the end of the grading period, students' goal attainment is evaluated using the goal attainment scale. When a goal has been attained, the students and teachers initiate the GOAL procedure again for the next marking period (Wehmeyer, Agran, & Hughes, 1998).

Goal setting was at the heart of the positive accomplishments domain at Geelong Grammar School. Positive accomplishments were defined as "the capacity to work toward meaningful goals, the motivation and grit to persist despite challenges and setbacks, and the achievement of competence and success in important life domains" (Norrish, 2015, p. 229). Pam Burton, a 5th grade teacher at Geelong, meets with students at the start of each term to support each student in setting at least three personal goals for the term. Students then create a visual representation of each goal, using a theme they choose. Themes include running a race and nearing the end or climbing a mountain and reaching the top. One visualization is that each student has a hot air balloon and basket. The balloon represents the goal, and each basket represents progress toward the goal. Every week, students move their basket closer to their balloon (their goal), so they have a visual representation of their progress. If their basket doesn't move, it provides Burton with a chance to talk about different options for making progress (Norrish, 2015, p. 239).

Teach Your Students to Engage in Planning

Planning is a future-focused, goal-oriented process linked to self-initiation and autonomy. Planning "provides a way to begin to act (self-initiate) by putting into play the motivational, cognitive, and emotional processes energized by autonomous motivation" (Shogren, Wehmeyer, & Khamsi, 2017, p. 211). Further, planning is an important part of the goal-setting process, and teaching planning skills is often incorporated into the goal-setting instruction process. The ideas of Pathway Thinking, introduced by Rick Snyder and colleagues in *Handbook of Hope* (Snyder, 2000), provide a structure for teaching planning skills. Snyder (1994) defined pathway thinking as "a cognitive sense of being able to generate routes to an envisioned goal" (p. 535). Hope Theory suggests that hope is a positive motivational state that is based upon goal-directed energy (agency thinking) and planning to meet goals (pathway thinking). This overlays with the Causal Agency Theory framework for promoting self-determined learning by focusing on promoting volitional and agentic action.

The idea of a "pathway" is helpful in teaching planning skills, both because it is an image one can use to help students visualize the planning process (e.g., a plan is a pathway from a goal to a desired outcome) and because looking down a path is a future-oriented activity. Snyder and colleagues (2000) noted that they find it useful "to have the children imagine that they are going on a trip . . . the goals they have set are their destinations, and they need to plot routes to reach those goals" (p. 47).

Steps in the pathways process that can be used to frame instruction include

1. Identify the goal for which planning will occur (e.g., the destination).
2. Break the goal down into objectives (e.g., steps along the pathway).
3. Identify multiple options (e.g., pathways) to achieve the goal and objectives.
4. Select the best option (e.g., choose to go down one path).
5. Determine the resources needed to implement the plan (e.g., supplies for the trip).
6. Create a timeline (e.g., schedule for the trip).
7. Create a tracking and evaluation process (e.g., mile markers down the path).
8. Evaluate progress and determine if the path is right or if another path is needed (e.g., whether you reached your destination).

They recommend that helping students build pathways involves dos and don'ts:

Do

- Teach students to have mental scripts about the chain of activities that occur in situations.
- Help students break a long pathway into smaller, doable steps.
- Teach students to think about failure as the result of ineffective strategies rather than a lack of talent.
- Talk with students about their plans for reaching their goals.

Don't

- Minimize students' concerns about something they have not learned (instead, offer help in addressing the problem).
- Require students to become quiet and submissive.
- Do all the planning for students.
- Readily agree with students if they conclude that there is no pathway available for reaching a goal. (p. 48)

And, we probably can't say enough that these strategies to promote volitional action are important, but that for them to translate to self-determined learning, such strategies must be in concert with emphasizing the importance of autonomy, competence, and relatedness supports; structuring learning environments and instructional materials to facilitate autonomy; using strengths-based approaches to facilitate mastery learning and competence beliefs; and providing optimal challenges that are self-endorsed and congruent with student values, interests, and passions. Many programs focus on goal-setting or problem-solving skills but fall short of achieving student ownership over learning and self-determined learning.

Teaching Agentic Action

Agentic action involves skills that enable one to direct and sustain action toward a goal. Figure 5.2 depicts areas of instruction to promote agentic action.

Promote Agentic Engagement Skills

An important element of student engagement is *agentic engagement*, discussed in the Research and Theory section that follows. Agentic engagement skills can be learned and, by learning and using these skills, students can influence the probability that they will be supported in self-determining learning. Put another way, through agentic engagement, "learners find ways of enriching, modifying, and personalizing their instruction" (Montenegro, 2017).

5.2 Component Elements of Agentic Action

Source: Adapted from Shogren, Raley, Burke, and Wehmeyer, 2019.

Research and Theory: Agentic Engagement Research

Reeve and Tseng have described agentic engagement as "students' constructive contribution into the flow of the instruction they receive" (p. 258). Think of it this way: traditionally, we think about student engagement as having behavioral (staying on task, working effortfully, persisting), emotional or motivational (interest, curiosity, enthusiasm), and cognitive (using learning strategies, self-regulating) elements (2011). All of that is what students are is doing when they are engaged. But research has shown that what students are doing also influences what teachers do. Teachers, when they see that their students are not engaged and seem disinterested and distracted, are likely to change what they're doing.

Ways in which teachers can teach students the skills leading to agentic engagement include

- Support students to think through and state their preferences and opinions about a topic or subject.

- Engage students to self-assess learning needs.
- Teach students to seek clarification on a topic or ask for an example.
- Encourage students to volunteer responses or to engage in activities.
- Maximize opportunities for all students in the class to speak and present.

Teach Your Students to Engage in Self-Regulated Learning

Self-regulation is a term that may have even more meanings than does the word *autonomy!* Most of us, though, have a general sense of what we mean by self-regulation. The Research and Theory section that follows provides information on how SDT and Self-Determined Learning Theory conceptualize self-regulation.

Research and Theory: Self-Regulation Conceptualization

Johnmarshall Reeve and colleagues in SDT research suggested that "self-regulation is a process in which people organize and manage their capacities—that is, their thoughts (e.g., competency beliefs), emotions (e.g., interest), behaviors (e.g., engagement with learning activities), and social-contextual surroundings (e.g., a quiet, comfortable place to study)—in the service of attaining some desired future state" (Reeve, Ryan, Deci, & Jang, 2012, p. 223).

Conceptualizing self-regulation within Self-Determined Learning Theory, Mithaug (1993) referred to self-regulation as how people "strive for and then maintain . . . the most optimal level of adjustment possible" (p. 52). When students are engaged in self-regulated learning, they organize and manage their resources (cognitive, metacognitive, emotional and motivational, behavioral) to act to solve problems to achieve goals related to learning and adjustment. That is, they engage in agentic action.

Dale Schunk and Barry Zimmerman are among the nation's leaders in self-regulated learning and have identified strategies to enable young people to self-regulate academic and educational action and performance. Keep in mind that self-regulated learning involves many of the processes we've already discussed, particularly goal-setting, problem-solving, and planning skills. Among the more frequently taught self-regulated learning strategies are self-assessment, self-instruction, self-monitoring, self-evaluation, and time management, summaries of which are presented in Figure 5.3.

5.3 Summary of Self-Regulation Strategies

Strategy	Description	Teaching Students the Strategy
Self-Assessment	Involves students assessing their own interests, preferences, and abilities; reflecting on their effort and performance; and identifying areas of instructional need. This typically occurs during the goal-setting process but can occur anywhere in the instructional process when students can identify information needed for instructional purposes.	1. Work with students to emphasize that self-assessment is intended to identify their own interests and preferences, what they know about a preferred outcome, and where they have particular areas of learning needs. 2. When a goal is set, support students in assessing what they currently know about the goal. 3. Teach students to reflect on questions that pertain to whether they understand their learning challenge, if they have the resources they need, and whether they are giving full effort to their work and, if not, why. 4. In addition to teaching students to self-monitor and self-evaluate their progress, teach them to identify when they need to know something they had not previously identified and to assess their learning needs in that area.
Self-Instruction	Involves teaching students to make task-specific self-instructions. It is basically teaching students to tell themselves what they need to do. These are generally not spoken aloud and usually relate more to a process than discrete steps in a specific task. That is, simply thinking "I did ___," "I need to do ____ next," and "now I am going to ___" (the Did-Next-Now strategy) enables students to organize and guide the process. Self-instruction is, essentially, a form of problem solving in which the student learns to think about what they've done, what they need to do, and how they will do it.	1. Work with students to understand a problem that they might encounter in the learning process. 2. Teach students a self-instruction strategy like Did-Next-Now to address the learning problem. 3. Teach students to state each step in a full sentence that incorporates the specific details of their task. 4. Encourage students to begin by quietly stating each step aloud.

continued

5.3 Summary of Self-Regulation Strategies *(continued)*

Strategy	Description	Teaching Students the Strategy
Self-Monitoring	Involves students monitoring their progress toward a goal. The strategy requires that students understand and successfully implement two functions—recognizing that the desired action, behavior, or outcome was successfully implemented, and accurately recording the occurrence in some way. Students can track progress toward the goal by recording outcomes when an activity is completed, recording in a specified time interval, or recording whatever is specified in the goal/objective. This data can be recorded in any way that works for students.	1. Ensure that the goal has measurable objectives and outcomes and that students understand those. 2. Work with students to develop a process to self-monitor progress. This typically involves using some means to chart or graph daily outcomes (e.g., checklists). 3. Ensure that students understand when to mark or count progress (e.g., end of a session, at an interval, or whatever is determined in the goal and action plan). 4. Ensure that students can discriminate the appropriate response or action.
Self-Evaluation	Involves the comparison of current progress toward the goal (provided by self-monitoring) with the desired goal state. It is an important part of the self-regulation process because it keeps students aware (on a regular basis) of progress toward the goal; thus it can provide motivation to pursue or to adjust one's action plan or the goal as needed.	1. Work with students to develop a means to evaluate data/information from self-monitoring process or other data sources. These usually involve pictorial representations (including graphs/charts, checklists, etc.). 2. Support students to compare current progress with desired progress. Again, using visual or pictorial representations like graphs/charts, tally sheets, checklists, and so forth will be helpful. 3. Work with students to identify if progress is adequate or if some change to the plan or goal is needed.
Time Management	Involves teaching students to successfully organize and manage time associated with learning tasks and activities. Time management is important in virtually any learning task (and, for that matter, life task!).	1. Teach students to create a plan (discussed previously) that breaks the goal down into manageable objectives and tasks. 2. Support students in estimating the time needed on learning tasks and activities. 3. Teach students to create a means to monitor time spent on a task and to revise their time estimates if needed. This can be a calendar or a timer (such as an app on a smartphone). 4. Teach students self-scheduling strategies that help them create learning schedules to identify when during the day they learn and work best, in what environmental contexts they learn effectively, and how to avoid distractions. 5. Teach students how to use to-do lists or task lists, such as those on calendaring software.

Source: From *A Teacher's Guide to Implementing the Self-Determined Learning Model of Instruction*, by M. L. Wehmeyer, M. Agran, S. B. Palmer, and D. E. Mithaug, 1999, Lawrence, KS: Beach Center on Disability. Copyright 1999 by Beach Center on Disability. Adapted with permission.

Typically, instruction in self-regulated learning combines most of the strategies in Figure 5.3. One research-based model that incorporates these elements is the Self-Regulated Strategy Development (SRSD) model. Developed by Karen Harris and Steve Graham (1992) to help teachers support students who struggle with writing, the model guides teachers to

- Help students to develop background knowledge about the learning goal and self-regulation strategies.
- Discuss the self-regulation strategy to be used with students to ensure they understand it, can use it, and can track their progress (self-monitor).
- Model the thinking processes students should use, the steps to the self-regulation strategy, and how to link this to the goal that has been set.
- Memorize the strategy processes and become more fluent with the strategy.
- Support students in practicing the strategy, including with peers and in small groups.
- Establish routines and processes that enable students to incorporate the strategy into their academic work (Harris & Graham, 1992).

SRSD has developed strategies like POW (Pick my idea, Organize my notes, Write and say more) and TREE (Topic, Reasons, Ending, Examine) that are basically self-instruction (and mnemonic) devices students can learn to improve their writing performance. But the process can be used in almost any content area.

Teach Your Students to Engage in Goal Attainment

Goal attainment involves the processes to sustain action toward a goal. Remember the New Year's Eve resolution problem? The reason why the majority of people do not reach the goals they set at the beginning of the year is related both to their skills at setting goals, as discussed, but also at attaining them. In the 1960s, cognitive psychologist George Miller proposed an influential explanation for goal attainment actions that is referred to as Test-Operate-Test-Exit, or just TOTE. Here is what Miller and colleagues said about the TOTE process:

> The general pattern of reflex action, therefore, is to test the input energies against some criteria established in the organism, to respond if the result of the test is to show an incongruity, and to continue to respond until the incongruity vanishes, at which time the reflex is terminated.

Thus, there is "feedback" from the result of the action to the testing phase, and we are confronted by a recursive loop. (Miller, Galanter, & Pribram, 1960, pp. 25–26)

Miller's model has been applied to information technology and artificial intelligence. But here's the basic thought: we learn to attain goals by "testing" where we are and what we know with regard to the goal state, continuing to work on it or alter what we're doing, testing again, and repeating that until we have reached our desired goal state. And how do we do that? Using the self-regulation strategies that we discussed in the previous section, by and large.

Teach Your Students to Advocate for Themselves and Others

Teaching students to advocate for their own interests and the interests of others they care about (self-advocacy skills) is important if they are to be successful in pursuing their passions. Such instruction involves

- Teaching skills and providing experiences related to leadership and teamwork.
- Teaching basic rights related to citizenship and legal rights.
- Teaching assertiveness and problem-resolution skills.
- Teaching public-speaking skills and use of community resources.

To begin with, students need to acquire a broader sense of themselves, learning to apply that knowledge to building a positive self-image and gaining self-confidence. To be self-aware, students should be taught to identify their basic physical and psychological needs, interests, and abilities. They should know which of these interests are common and which are unique. Students should also know how their behavior affects others to be self-aware.

Students need to be able to be assertive to express their opinions and make their wishes known. This concept of assertiveness is between aggressiveness and passivity; students need to learn how to express their positive and negative feelings appropriately, to initiate and terminate conversations when needed, and to say "no" if that is what they truly wish to say.

The Self-Determined Learning Model of Instruction

In our own work to promote student ownership and self-determined learning, we asked a seemingly simple question that, at the time, did not have many simple answers. That question was "What can we do to teach teachers to teach students to teach themselves?" But when we looked at widely used teaching models, all of them were models that enabled teachers to teach students, not to enable teachers to teach students to teach themselves. Teachers use many models of teaching—role-playing, direct instruction, and social learning models, to name a few—in the course of any given day, depending on the content and the context (Joyce & Weil, 1980). The resulting teaching model, called the Self-Determined Learning Model of Instruction (SDLMI) (Wehmeyer et al., 1999) provides teachers with a model to support self-determined learning.

The model enables teachers to teach students to self-regulate problem solving to set a goal, create an action plan, and adjust the action plan or goal as needed so that they can achieve the goal. The model operationalizes all of the elements in Causal Agency Theory and incorporates aspects of every teaching strategy we've discussed in this chapter. The model has strong evidence of its beneficial use with adolescents who are struggling to learn but is viable for all students. It can be used by teachers to teach students to self-determine learning in any content or topic area. Figures 5.4, 5.5, and 5.6 provide a flow chart for the model.

The model is implemented across three phases. Each phase poses a problem for the student to solve using the following questions: "What is my goal?", "What is my plan?", and "What have I learned?" Teachers teach students to solve these problems by answering a series of questions. The student questions vary by phase but comprise a four-step problem-solving sequence. Aligned with each student question are teacher objectives, which are objectives a teacher will be trying to accomplish by implementing the model. Also grouped by teacher objective are educational supports that teachers may use to enable students to learn what they need to answer each question.

Instruction during the first phase (see Figure 5.4) teaches students to solve the problem, "What is my goal?" and to define the discrepancy between what they know and what they want to know. The questions posed in this phase assist students in setting a goal that will lead them to what they want to know. The last question in that phase asks, "What can I do to make this happen?" and students are supported to set a goal.

Figure 5.5 depicts the second phase of the model, in which students solve the problem, "What is my plan?" The questions in this phase support students in defining the discrepancy between the action that is necessary to learn what they want to know and the actions they are capable of taking and to engage in pathways thinking to create a plan. This phase ends with students having developed a plan of action and designing a self-monitoring process.

5.4 Phase 1 of Self-Determined Learning Model of Instruction

Self-Determined Learning Model of Instruction
Phase 1: Set a Goal
Student Problem to Solve: What is my goal?

Student Questions

Teacher Objectives
And Primary Educational Supports*

1. What do I want to learn?

1a. **Enable student to identify specific strengths and instructional needs**
   • Student self-assessment of interests, abilities, and instructional needs
1b. **Enable student to communicate preferences, interests, beliefs, and values**
   • Communication instruction
1c. **Enable student to prioritize needs**
   • Decision-making instruction, problem-solving instruction

2. What do I know about it now?

2a. **Enable student to identify current status in relation to the instructional need**
   • Problem-solving instruction, decision-making instruction
2b. **Enable student to gather information about opportunities and barriers in their environments**
   • Awareness instruction, self-advocacy instruction

3. What must change for me to learn what I don't know?

3a. **Enable student to decide if actions will be focused on capacity building, modifying the environment, or both**
   • Decision-making instruction, problem-solving instruction
3b. **Enable student to choose a need to address from the prioritized list**
   • Choice-making instruction

4. What can I do to make this happen?

4a. **Enable student to state a goal and identify criteria for achieving goal**
   • Goal-setting instruction

Go to Phase 2

* In addition to the Primary Educational Supports, other supports may be used as needed. See the *SDLMI Teacher's Guide* for more information.

Source: Shogren, Raley, Burke, and Wehmeyer, 2019.

5.5 Phase 2 of Self-Determined Learning Model of Instruction

Self-Determined Learning Model of Instruction
Phase 2: Take Action
Student Problem to Solve: What is my plan?

Student Questions

Teacher Objectives
And Primary Educational Supports*

5. **What can I do to learn what I don't already know?**

5a. **Enable student to self-evaluate current status and self-identified goal status**
   • Goal-attainment instruction

6. **What could keep me from taking action?**

6a. **Enable student to determine plan of action to bridge gap between self-evaluated current status and self-identified goal status**
   • Self-monitoring instruction, self-evaluation instruction

7. **What can I do to remove these barriers?**

7a. **Collaborate with student to identity appropriate instructional strategies**
   • Communication instruction
7b. **Teach student needed student-directed learning strategies**
   • Antecedent cue regulation instruction
7c. **Support student to implement student-directed learning strategies**
   • Self-instruction, self-scheduling instruction
7d. **Provide mutually agreed-upon teacher-directed instruction**
   • Choice-making instruction

8. **When will I take action?**

8a. **Enable student to determine schedule for action plan**
   • Self-scheduling instruction
8b. **Enable student to implement action plan**
   • Self-instruction
8c. **Enable student to self-monitor progress**
   • Self-monitoring instruction

Go to Phase 3

* In addition to the Primary Educational Supports, other supports may be used as needed. See the *SDLMI Teacher's Guide* for more infromation.

Source: Shogren, Raley, Burke, and Wehmeyer, 2019.

Figure 5.6 depicts the third and final phase of the model, in which students solve the problem, "What have I learned?" and, in so doing, examine the discrepancy between their planned actions and the actions they've implemented and between what they expected to learn and what they learned. Students use information they've gathered through their self-monitoring to self-evaluate progress and, supported by the questions in the phase, go through a decision-making process to determine if their progress is sufficient (and, if so, keep working on it as they have been) or if they need to alter their plan or goal.

Raley, Shogren, and McDonald (2018) tell the story of two teachers in high school who have concluded that their students need to learn to be more self-determined. One teacher, Ms. Elliott, is an algebra teacher with more than 25 years of experience. The second teacher, Mr. Dupont, is a special educator supporting students with learning disabilities in Ms. Elliott's algebra class. He has implemented the SDLMI in other contexts, and together they decide that all of the students in each of Ms. Elliott's algebra class sections could benefit from learning how to set and attain goals and to learn more autonomously. Ms. Elliott identified the biggest barriers to student success in her classes as being related to working more productively independently, having the right materials, and finishing assignments in a timely manner. These are, fundamentally, planning, goal-setting, problem-solving, and self-regulating issues. Together, Ms. Elliott and Mr. Dupont taught all the students taking algebra the steps to the model. What they found was that students were better able to self-determine learning after just one semester of teaching students using the SDLMI. They are now talking to the English teachers in the high school about using the SDLMI to support students to self-determine learning in those sections.

The Research to Practice section that closes this chapter provides a summary of teaching strategies for student ownership and self-determined learning. In Chapter 6, we turn our attention to assessment and technology to promote student ownership and self-determined learning.

5.6 Phase 3 of Self-Determined Learning Model of Instruction

Self-Determined Learning Model of Instruction
Phase 3: Adjust Goal or Plan
Student Problem to Solve: What have I learned?

Student Questions

Teacher Objectives
And Primary Educational Supports*

9. **What actions have I taken?**

9a. **Enable student to self-evaluate progress toward goal achievement**
   • Self-evaluating instruction, self-recording instruction

10. **What barriers have been removed?**

10a. **Collaborate with student to compare progress with desired outcomes**
   • Self-monitoring instruction, self-evaluation instruction

11. **What has changed about what I don't know?**

11a. **Support student to re-evaluate goal if progress is insufficient**
   • Goal-attainment instruction
11b. **Assist student to decide if goal should remain the same or change**
   • Decision-making instruction
11c. **Collaborate with student to identify if action plan is adequate or inadequate given revised or retained goal**
   • Self-evaluation instruction
11d. **Enable student to choose a need to address from the prioritized list**
   • Choice-making instruction

12. **Do I know what I want to know?**

12a. **Enable student to decide if progress is adequate, inadequate, or if goal has been achieved**
   • Self-evaluation instruction, self-reinforcement instruction

* In addition to the Primary Educational Supports, other supports may be used as needed. See the *SDLMI Teacher's Guide* for more information.

Source: Shogren, Raley, Burke, and Wehmeyer, 2019.

Research to Practice: Strategies for Student Ownership and Self-Determined Learning

Engaging students in opportunities to learn, practice, and implement skills pertaining to *volitional action* and *agentic action,* combined with the general principles of student ownership and self-determined learning related to autonomy, competence, and relatedness supports, leads to the development of *action-control beliefs* that support students' efforts to act as causal agents.

Teaching Volitional Action

To act volitionally, students must use skills that enable them to initiate and engage in causal action, including problem-solving, decision-making, goal-setting, and planning skills.

Solving problems is essential if students are to engage in self-determined learning. If you already know something, you don't need to learn it. If you don't know something, that is, by definition, a problem. Teaching problem solving focuses on five steps

1. Problem orientation;
2. Problem definition and formulation;
3. Generation of alternative solutions;
4. Decision making; and
5. Solution implementation.

A decision is a process that begins by solving a problem. It involves weighing the consequences involved with various decision options; taking into account one's preferences, interests, values, and beliefs; and, ultimately choosing one of the options. Developmentally, children acquire the requisite skills for decision making in early adolescence, after they have learned how to solve problems.

Skills to teach in the decision-making process include:

- Recognition of the circumstances that lead to the need for a decision.
- Awareness of the need to make a decision.
- Identification of the goal in which the decision is in service.
- Identification of action alternatives.
- Determination of the consequences of each action alternative.
- Determination of the probability of each consequence occurring if action is undertaken.
- Establishment of the relative importance (value or utility) of each action alternative and consequence.
- Integration of the probability and importance determination to identify the most attractive course of action.

Setting a goal regulates our actions. When we set a goal, we're more likely to expend resources to address the goal.

Fundamentally, there are four steps in teaching goal setting:

1. Identifying and enunciating goals.
2. Developing objectives to meet goals.
3. Identifying actions necessary to achieve goals.
4. Tracking and following progress on goals.

Teaching goal identification and enunciation involves teaching students to state goals in ways that make them achievable, including having clear, measurable outcomes. The action planning process includes the development of objectives and actions to meet the goal. Every student can be involved in tracking and following their own progress toward a goal, thus improving autonomous motivation.

Planning is a future-focused, goal-oriented process linked to self-initiation and autonomy and is an important part of the goal-setting process.

Teach students "pathways thinking" that involves

- Identifying the goal for which planning will occur (e.g., the destination).
- Breaking the goal down into objectives (e.g., steps along the pathway).
- Identifying multiple options (e.g., pathways) to achieve the goal and objectives.
- Selecting the best option (e.g., choosing to go down one path).
- Determining resources needed to implement plan (e.g., supplies for the trip).
- Creating a timeline (e.g., schedule for the trip).
- Creating a tracking and evaluation process (e.g., mile markers down the path).
- Evaluating progress and determining if the path is right or if another path is needed (e.g., if you reached your destination).

Teaching Agentic Action

Agentic action involves skills that enable one to direct and sustain action toward a goal: promoting agentic engagement

Agentic engagement refers to the students' contribution to the flow of instruction they receive; responding to educators, asking questions, and autonomously engaging in the learning process. Educators can promote agentic engagement skills by

- Supporting students to think through and state their preferences and opinions about a topic or subject.
- Engaging students to self-assess learning needs.
- Teaching students to seek clarification on a topic or ask for an example.
- Encouraging students to volunteer responses or to engage in activities.
- Maximizing opportunities for all students in the class to speak and present.

Self-regulation involves those skills that enable learners to organize and manage their resources (cognitive, metacognitive, emotional, motivational, behavioral) to act to solve problems to achieve goals related to learning and adjustment.

Among the more frequently taught self-regulated learning strategies are self-assessment, self-instruction, self-monitoring, self-evaluation, and time management.

Goal-attainment skills are required to sustain action toward a goal after it has been set. This is a process of "testing" where we are and what we know with regard to the goal and involves ongoing implementation of self-regulation strategies.

Teaching students to advocate for their own interests and the interests of others they care about is important if they are to be successful in pursuing their passions. Such instruction involves:

continued

Research to Practice: Strategies for Student Ownership and Self-Determined Learning
(*continued*)

- Teaching skills and providing experiences related to leadership and teamwork.
- Teaching basic rights related to citizenship and legal rights.
- Teaching assertiveness and problem-resolution skills.
- Teaching public speaking skills and use of community resources.

The Self-Determined Learning Model of Instruction is an evidence-based teaching model that enables teachers to teach students to set a goal, create an action plan, and adjust their action plan or goal as needed so that students can achieve goals.

The model is implemented across three phases. Each phase poses a problem for the student to solve via the following questions:

- What is my goal?
- What is my plan?
- What have I learned?

Teachers teach students to solve these problems by answering a series of questions. The student questions, which vary by phase, comprise a four-step problem-solving sequence.

Assessment and Technology for Student Ownership and Self-Determined Learning

The originators of Self-Determination Theory (SDT), which we discussed in Chapter 2, have observed that, fundamentally, a standardized curriculum, high-stakes testing, accountability approach to education is nothing more or less than a motivation strategy. Deci and Ryan (2016) wrote

> By applying rewards and sanctions to districts, schools, and teachers based on a narrow set of student performances, the idea is to incentivize students, teachers, and schools to improve on these indicators. (p. 10)

But, they argue

> This controlling approach actually involves incentivizing, reinforcing, or rewarding *outcomes* rather than *behaviors*. (p. 10)

And what outcomes are incentivized? Standardized, routinized, predetermined outcomes.

As Zhao (2018b) stated, "the education system rarely cares about children's individual passions or talents" and that "with very few exceptions, schools generally do not ask what students are good at, interested in, or passionate about" (p. 17). But if we are to shift to an education system that emphasizes student ownership and self-determined learning, this is exactly what we have to do—ask what students are good at, interested in, and passionate about. We have to design and implement assessments that test more than outcomes and, indeed, provide information that informs progress and growth.

Assessment for Student Ownership and Self-Determined Learning

Strengths-Based Assessments

Recall the discussion about the Geelong Grammar School in Australia. Among the measures that are collected are those that focus on student well-being and positive mental health: resilience, confidence in achieving goals, life satisfaction, happiness, gratitude, and perseverance (Vella-Brodrick et al., 2014). Similarly, assessment to facilitate student ownership and self-determined learning should focus on student beliefs, characteristics, and well-being, as well as inform growth and progress pertaining to self-determined learning. It should be future-oriented in that it is intended not to evaluate but to provide information to facilitate progress and self-direction. It should employ multiple measurement techniques, beginning with active student participation in assessment. And it should empower students.

What does this look like? There are a host of positive psychological assessments that can provide information about students' well-being, resiliency, and so forth. Margaret Kern, a pioneer in positive education at the Centre for Positive Psychology at The University of Melbourne, has focused on providing tools and measures to assess PERMA—the acronym for Martin Seligman's model for psychological elements that need to be maximized to achieve a life of happiness and well-being (Seligman, 2011), the elements of which are

- Positive emotion
- Engagement
- Relationships
- Meaning
- Accomplishments

These elements should sound very familiar as important for self-determined learning: meaningfulness, autonomy, competence, relatedness . . . a focus on self-determined learning necessitates a focus on PERMA.

St. Peter's College in Adelaide, Australia—a school for boys grades R–12 (R refers to reception year and is the year before grade one, comparable to kindergarten)—has adopted the PERMA format to structure positive education. Kern and colleagues have developed, for example, the

EPOCH Measure of Adolescent Well-Being (Kern, Benson, Steinberg, & Steinberg, 2015) that is in use at St. Peter's. The scale measures *Engagement*, *Perseverance*, *Optimism*, *Connectedness*, and *Happiness*. The EPOCH measures are student self-reported, so the student is the agent in assessing and interpreting information.

Another measure implemented at St. Peter's and widely available is the Children's Hope Scale (Snyder et al., 1997). Snyder was the originator of Hope Theory, which defines hope not as a wish but as a motivational state "based on an interactively derived sense of successful (a) agency (goal-directed energy) and (b) pathways (planning to meet goals)" (Snyder, 2000, p. 8). We discussed Hope Theory and Pathways Thinking in Chapter 5. The Children's Hope Scale is a very short, student self-reported measure of agency and pathways. Research using the Children's Hope Scale has found that hope is highly, positively related to better academic performance, reduced anxiety and self-deprecatory thinking in academic situations, and a positive problem-solving orientation (Marques & Lopez, 2017).

Although not widely used in schools, there are a host of questionnaires and measures related to the characteristics and attributes of positive education and well-being. The Positive Psychology Center at the University of Pennsylvania is a pioneer in the development and dissemination of these tools, many of which you can access (at no cost) at https://www.authentichappiness.sas.upenn.edu/testcenter.

Another online resource is the VIA Institute of Character. The VIA Youth Survey is one of several online assessments of character strengths. The original VIA Classification of Strengths was developed by Martin Seligman and his colleague Chris Peterson from the University of Pennsylvania (Peterson & Seligman, 2004). The VIA tools assess a person's 24 character strengths, organized into six overarching virtues—wisdom, courage, humanity, justice, temperance, and transcendence.

The VIA character strengths include such areas as creativity, honesty, kindness, bravery, social intelligence, teamwork, fairness, leadership, humility, gratitude, and hope, all organized under the six virtues. The VIA Youth Survey is a 96-item student self-directed assessment of these 24 character strengths for youth ages 10 to 17. Assessment provides information on five signature strengths; that is, those character strengths on which the student scored highest. Teachers, in turn, can use this information to structure learning contexts to take advantage of student strengths. A frequent strategy utilizing this information is called "use your signature strengths in new ways each day," and just the name makes this a fairly self-evident strategy! In one 5th grade classroom, all students took the VIA Youth Survey. Each morning, the teacher would post one of each student's signature strengths, and the student would exhibit that strength three times during the day. Imagine, a full day of students practicing kindness, humility, humor, creativity, honesty, fairness, and the like! We know students have these virtues; it's just that school doesn't often provide opportunities for them to be recognized. Another strategy that was used in the Geelong Grammar School was strengths-spotting, where students spot character strengths in their peers. The VIA Youth Survey is freely available online at http://www.viacharacter.org, and there is also a supplement for use to support youth with disabilities to complete the assessment (Shogren, Wehmeyer, Forber-Pratt, & Palmer, 2015). Psychologist Ryan Niemiec has pioneered interventions to promote each of the 24 character strengths (2017).

Assessments for Self-Determined Learning

Assessments of PERMA and positive education provide useful tools to emphasize students' strengths, well-being, interests, and passions. There are, however, tools more specific to the self-determined learning context and process that teachers can use. To begin with, there are a number of assessments associated with SDT that are available online through the CSDT portal (https://selfdeterminationtheory.org/) and that assist in understanding students' perceptions of choice and autonomy. For example, the Perceived Choice and Awareness of Self Scale (Sheldon & Deci, 1993) measures the degree to which a person feels a sense of choice with regard to an action. The Index of Autonomous Functioning (Weinstein, Przybylski, & Ryan, 2012) is a brief measure of a person's perceptions of authorship/self-congruence, interest-taking, and low susceptibility to control—in other words, perceived autonomy. The Academic Self-Regulation Questionnaire (Ryan & Connell, 1989), developed for students in late elementary and middle school, measures why students engage in various school-related activities and whether they are externally regulated or intrinsically motivated. An adapted version has been validated for use with students with learning disabilities (Deci, Hodges, Pierson, & Tomassone, 1992). The Agentic Engagement Scale (Reeve, 2013) is used to measure the extent to which students constructively contribute to the instruction they receive.

There are other tools available; these just give you a sense of what is out there. One more assessment that measures self-determination is also freely available online: The Self-Determination Inventory: Student Report (SDI:SR) (Shogren et al., 2017) is a self-report measure of self-determination that operationalizes Causal Agency Theory, as discussed in Chapter 3. Specifically, the SDI:SR is a 21-item self-report measure that provides information on student volitional action, agentic action, and action-control beliefs. The SDI:SR provides measures of each of the three essential characteristics—volitional action, agentic action, action-control beliefs—and nine component constructs—autonomy, self-initiation, pathways thinking, self-regulation, self-direction, agentic thinking, control expectancy beliefs, causality beliefs, and agency beliefs. Normed with adolescents and young adults ages 13 to 21 with and without disabilities, the SDI:SR is taken online (at http://www.self-determination.org) and includes accessibility features that enable younger adolescents and students with learning difficulties to complete it. Findings provide information for students and teachers to identify areas of instructional need related to self-determination and support young people to acquire knowledge and skills that enable them to better self-determine learning.

These tools and many more are available (most at no or low cost) to support efforts to change how assessments are is used and to promote self-determined learning. Such assessments will contribute to instructional strategies identified in Chapter 5 and can provide information that is future focused, participant driven, and empowering.

Technology for Student Ownership and Self-Determined Learning

Technology has for a long time been used to improve education in a variety of ways (Cuban, 1993, 2001; Zhao et al., 2015). Despite its potential to transform education (Papert, 1993, 1999), technology has failed to do so because the primary use of technology in education has been to improve the current paradigm (Zhao et al., 2015). In fact, in many ways, technology has worked to strengthen the traditional paradigm by providing more powerful tools to impose control over students' learning through more convenient and effective data collection and monitoring. MIT professor and inventor Mitchel Resnick (2017) observed that "the same pedagogical approach [is] repeated decades later, with greater efficiency, thanks to new technologies" (p. 23). The late MIT professor and pioneer of educational technology Seymour Papert once quipped that using technology in the traditional paradigm is akin to using a jet engine to drive a horse wagon. Unless the horse wagon is broken, the power of the jet engine cannot be unleashed.

From Hole-in-the-Wall to Granny Cloud

Sugata Mitra's Hole-in-the-Wall experiments mark a dramatic departure from traditional uses of technology. In 1999, Mitra, a professor at the UK's University of Newcastle, and his colleagues placed a computer into the opening of a wall in the slum of New Delhi, India. The computer was connected to the Internet and had a number of programs. The computer screen was visible from the street and anyone could use the computer. But there were no instructions as to how to use the computer. "What happened next astonished us," recounted (Mitra, 2012b):

> Children came running out of the nearest slum and glued themselves to the computer. They couldn't get enough. They began to click and explore. They began to learn how to use this strange thing. A few hours later, a visibly surprised Vivek said the children were actually surfing the web.

More astonishment was in store. The computer was left in the hole on the wall and available to everyone who passed by, "and within six months the children of the neighborhood had learned all the mouse operations, could open and close programs, and were going online to download games, music, and videos" (Mitra, 2012b).

Mitra repeated the experiment in two other locations in India and had the same result. Children all learned how to use the computer without being taught. "Language did not matter and neither did education," wrote Mitra. After hundreds of similar experiments in different locations and cultures over a decade (Wilby, 2016), Mitra found that each and every time "the children were able to develop deep learning by teaching themselves" (Mitra, 2012b).

Out of the Hole-in-the-Wall project, Mitra developed the concept of the self-organized learning environment or SOLE. SOLE is also referred to as School in the Cloud, which essentially is expanding the hole in the wall to a larger venue: a school. In 2013, Mitra won a $1 million prize to build his School in the Cloud to expand the idea that children, with access to a networked computer, can essentially learn by themselves. The School in the Cloud connects children in poor and rural parts of India to "grannies"—volunteers in the UK and elsewhere who may or may not be actual grandmothers but who are willing to interact with children in the School in the Cloud via Skype. "The role of the Granny includes provoking curiosity, asking questions, listening attentively, and providing warm encouragement" (The Granny Cloud, n.d.).

The significance of the School in the Cloud may be discounted as simply a way to provide education to children in places where there are an insufficient number of high-quality teachers. In and of itself this is already very significant because too many children in the world today do not have access to high-quality teachers. But the significance goes way beyond connecting poor children to remote learning resources through technology. Such has been done for a long time, from traditional distance-education programs delivered via radio and TV to the recent Massive Open Online Courses or MOOC movement (Bonk, Lee, Reeves, & Reynolds, 2015; Cuban, 1986; Pappano, 2012).

What makes the Hole-in-the-Wall and the School-in-the-Cloud experiments truly significant is the education approach they employed. Instead of following the traditional approach, like MOOCs or distance-education programs, of offering prescribed and predetermined teaching to students, these experiments did not have teachers or instructors in the traditional sense. Instead, the children were the owners of their learning. They exercised self-determination over their learning. They decided what they were interested in learning and directed their own learning. The computer or the "grannies" did not determine or dictate what and how children learned nor did they assess the outcomes of learning against some standards.

In many ways, SOLE is an essential approach to self-determined education with the support of technology. It was indeed Mitra's intention to use technology to transform education because he believed that the "SOLE method, or child-directed self-learning, is about acquiring the skills that people need in today's world: how to research information, evaluate sources, work in teams," wrote Carole Cadwalladr (2015), a journalist who interviewed Mitra for the UK newspaper *The Guardian* (Cadwalladr, 2015). It does not have to be only for children in poor and remote areas where qualified teachers are typically not available. It can be used as a way to transform education, to realize self-determined education anywhere. In fact, it has been implemented in developed countries such as the UK and shown its power (Cadwalladr, 2015; Wilby, 2016). There are thousands of SOLEs around the world today (Cadwalladr, 2015).

The Children's Machine

Mitra's experiments show that the power of modern technology for education can only be realized in a new education paradigm. Zhao and colleagues discuss the top five mistakes in educational technology in their book, *Never Send a Human to Do a Machine's Job: Correcting the Top*

5 Mistakes in Ed Tech (2015). One of the mistakes is treating technology as a teaching tool used by educators, which has proven to be problematic in many ways, such as wasting teachers' time on learning the technology and limiting the realization of the educational potentials of technology). To correct this mistake, Zhao and colleagues argue that technology should belong to the children. It's the children's machine, not the teachers', the late MIT professor Seymour Papert argued in his book, *The Children's Machine: Rethinking School in the Age of the Computer* (1993).

In self-determined education, the ownership of technology in schools is returned to the children. The child, instead of the teacher, determines when and how to use technology to learn, as well as what to learn. The ownership of technology can only be returned to children when the ownership of learning is returned to them. In other words, when children own their learning, they can determine how to use technology to support their learning.

Technology for Inquiry

Children can use technology to find answers to their questions. Today the Internet has become ubiquitous. Today's children are growing up with continuous connectivity to the Internet. The Internet has become an ever-growing source of information from which anyone, children included, can seek answers to their questions. They can search for answers to their questions from all sorts of existing information collections such as ancient texts, scholarly and scientific publications, government and legal documents, museum websites, technical manuals, DIY videos, and the like. They can also take online courses for more systematic studies of a subject from Khan Academy, Coursera, edX, or other MOOCs for free and courses from online schools and universities.

The Internet is not only a collection of information. It brings together a huge collection of people. As of June 2018, a total of 3.2 billion people —or more than 55 percent of the world's population—had access to the Internet, according to the Internet World Stats website (2019). This means, technically, a student with Internet access can communicate with 3.2 billion people who are scattered around the world. Consequently, students can learn from or with that many people. Their source of learning is no longer confined to the adults in their immediate physical environment. If a student cannot find answers to their questions from existing documents, they can ask someone online, as demonstrated by the Granny Cloud. As Mitra observed

A few years ago, nobody had a piece of plastic to which they could ask questions and have it answer back. The Greeks spoke of the Oracle of Delphi. We've created it. People don't talk to a machine. They talk to a huge collective of people, a kind of hive (Cadwalladr, 2015).

A huge collective of people make it a reality that, for many children today, practically anything can be learned from anyone anywhere in the world. As a result, the possibility of self-determined education is vastly expanded thanks to technology. Schools, wherever they are located, can and should no longer limit the subjects of learning to what they can offer within the boundaries of the school.

Technology for Collaboration

Technology is not only a tool for getting answers from the Internet. It is also a powerful tool for students to seek peer collaborators and partners in learning beyond their immediate physical environment. This is of particular importance in self-determined education. We know that learning is social, and children appreciate social connections and recognition in learning activities. But when students pursue their own learning, it may be the case that the subject of learning of some children is not shared by their peers in their immediate class or school, making it difficult for them to find like-minded peers to work with. The huge collective of people makes it possible for students, no matter how uncommon their interests, to find someone with similar interests.

Finding people with similar interests and passions is crucial for children for a number of reasons. First, it helps to assure them that their unique pursuit is not abnormal or weird because there are many others who share their interests and passions. Second, it enables learners to engage in collaborative or cooperative learning with people from different cultures and situations. Although learners may have a similar interest in learning something, their different cultural backgrounds can bring varied perspectives to the topic of common interest and thus enhance learning. Finally, learning with people with similar interests who are located in different parts of the world broadens the student's perspectives and helps develop cross-cultural communication and collaboration skills, which is an essential quality in the age of globalization.

Technology has also made collaboration over long distances very easy. Video and audio conferencing systems are readily available for synchronous meetings. Cloud-based collaboration tools, such as Google's G Suite for Education, make collaboration across time and distance effortless.

Social media platforms such as Twitter, Facebook, and Instagram provide powerful tools for community building.

Technology for Creation

Self-determined education is about enabling each and every child to realize their individual potential to become uniquely great, develop their creativity, and foster their entrepreneurial spirit (Zhao, 2018a, 2018b). Technology has the potential to help children access expertise and peers from a distance to pursue their unique greatness. It can also help children develop creativity and entrepreneurial spirit through creating authentic products and services that are of value to others (Zhao, 2012, 2018b).

Using technology to facilitate deep learning and creativity through constructing meaningful objects has a long tradition. For example, manipulatives have been used to facilitate math learning for young children for a long time (Laski, Jor'dan, Daoust, & Murray, 2015). The emergence of digital technology has greatly expanded the capacity of technology to engage children in creative construction. The pioneering work of Seymour Papert and colleagues at the MIT media lab began to explore the power of technology in facilitating deep learning and cultivating creativity in the 1980s (Harel & Papert, 1991; Kafai & Resnick, 1996; Resnick, 2017).

That tradition has grown tremendously over the past few decades. Most notably, Resnick, who was a student of Papert's, created the Scratch software language that has enabled millions of children to create interactive stories, games, music, and art. Technological tools such as Scratch create environments that support children's development of creativity because "[t]he key challenge is not how to 'teach creativity' to children, but rather how to create a fertile environment in which their creativity will take root, grow, and flourish," as Resnick (2017) writes in his book, *Lifelong Kindergarten: Cultivating Creativity through Projects, Passion, Peers, and Play* (p. 168).

Scratch is not the only environment enabled by technology to foster creativity. There are many other technological tools that can be used to facilitate the development of creativity in children. Students can use animation software to create 2D or 3D animated stories or films. They can also use easily available video software and cameras that come with smartphones to make movies. They can make art, music, and games using software other than Scratch. They can create physical objects using 3D printers or laser cutters. The power of technology for children to create is limitless, and it comes at much more affordable prices than ever before.

Technology has made it possible for children to easily make their creations available to billions of people. Their writings can be easily published on a website or social media platform, which is instantly accessible to a worldwide audience. They can share their photos, music, artwork, and videos with anyone in the world. They can as well make their physical products available to a global market of consumers.

Making products available to others vastly expands the opportunity for entrepreneurial learning. Entrepreneurship is essentially creating value for others. It is about solving other people's problems or bettering other people's lives with services and products. Thus, entrepreneurial learning needs an audience or customers. Technology enlarges the potential size of an audience and customer base, making it possible for children to find people who may need their products or services.

Technology for Assessment and Organization

Students can also utilize technology to organize, manage, assess, and present their self-determined learning experiences. Digital technology is a powerful tool for collecting, organizing, and presenting information in various flexible modalities. In self-determined education, students need to learn to organize and manage their personalized learning plans, which are co-constructed with adults (teachers and parents). They need to collect and present artifacts that demonstrate their learning and assess their progress. These artifacts can be in a wide range of formats and modalities depending on their strengths and interests. For those interested in art, for example, the artifacts may be paintings, while for those interested in film making, the artifacts can be videos. For students pursuing creative writing, the artifacts would be writing samples. Whatever formats or modalities the artifacts may take, students can assemble them into digital portfolios and present them to other stakeholders, such as teachers and parents, for assessment and feedback.

Students can also use technology to manage their own learning environments. There are all sorts of technological tools that help with daily tasks, such as scheduling, so that students can better manage their time and track tasks. There are also online tools for students to manage their contacts, which is helpful for students in managing collaboration with others. Additionally, students can use technology to organize and manage their learning resources such as websites, video collections, and electronic books.

Adults, teachers, school administrators, parents, and other interested parties can use technology to help students manage their own learning. Cloud-based applications and collaboration platforms enable adults to co-participate in students' learning. They can monitor students' progress against the co-constructed personalized learning plans, remind students of upcoming tasks, provide feedback on students' work, and suggest additional learning resources.

The Dark Side of Technology

While technology holds tremendous educational potential, it has a dark side. It can alienate children from nature. It can lead to addictions of all sorts—addiction to video games, social media, texting, and binge watching online videos, to name a few. It provides a platform for cyberbullying. It can damage eyesight and lead to other health issues, as a result of the lack of physical movement caused by excessive use of technology. It can lead to shallow processing of information. It can lead students to biased or untrue information. As a result, there is much discussion about limiting students' "screen time" and banning the use of smart devices in schools.

While the dark side of technology exists, the solution cannot be simplistically limiting or banning its use altogether. Technolgy is a powerful tool and banning its use is like throwing the baby out with the bath water, and, in a technological society, children cannot truly avoid technology. A more productive approach is to help children develop digital competency—capacities to live productively and healthily in the digital world (Zhao, 2009b).

The ability to use technology responsibly and productively can be effectively developed through self-determined education. When children use technology to support their own learning, they have autonomy, which is always accompanied with responsibility. Thus they need to figure out how to use technology productively and responsibly to accomplish their learning goals. They do not have to spend time and energy evading adult supervision and monitoring. As Mitchel Resnick (2017) points out:

> Rather than trying to minimize screen time, I think parents and teachers should try to maximize creative time. The focus shouldn't be on which technologies children are using, but rather what children are doing with them. (p. 25)

Returning Assessment and Technology to the Student

Assessment is always a concern when it comes to enabling self-determined learning. It is natural that parents, educators, and the public have a strong interest in knowing whether children are learning the right things and making the right amount of progress. But the traditional paradigm of assessment, which has co-evolved with the traditional paradigm of education, is obsolete. It is rooted in the tradition of judging individual students against predetermined standards and averages of a group (Rose, 2016; Zhao, 2016b). It also assesses knowledge acquisition but fails to consider other more important outcomes, such as uniqueness, creativity, and entrepreneurial thinking (Zhao, 2016a, 2018e). The new paradigm of education requires a new paradigm of assessment. In this chapter, we have discussed the new paradigm of assessment and presented a number of tools for assessment in self-determined learning.

Technology, particularly digital technology, has great potential to transform education and learning. The ever-growing power of technology, however, can only be harnessed in a new paradigm of education—self-determined education. Reciprocally, self-determined education can benefit greatly from technology. We have presented a number of ways that technology can be used to enable and support self-determined education. The key is to return the ownership of technology to children.

The Research to Practice section that concludes this chapter summarizes the important roles of assessment and technology in promoting student ownership and self-determined learning. In Chapter 7, the final chapter, we take a look at how to pull all of this together to achieve student ownership and self-determined learning.

Research to Practice: Assessment and Technology for Student Ownership and Self-Determined Learning

If we are to shift to an education system that emphasizes student ownership and self-determined learning, we have to begin to ask what students are good at, interested in, and passionate about.

Assessment to facilitate student ownership and self-determined learning should

- Focus on student beliefs, characteristics, and well-being.
- Inform growth and progress pertaining to self-determined learning.
- Be future-oriented (i.e., provide information to facilitate progress and self-direction, not evaluate).
- Employ multiple measurement techniques, beginning with active student participation in assessment.
- Empower students.

continued

Research to Practice: Assessment and Technology for Student Ownership and Self-Determined Learning (*continued*)

There are a host of positive psychological assessments that can provide information about students' well-being, resiliency, and so forth. Tools and measures designed to assess PERMA have been provided. The elements of PERMA are

- *Positive emotion*
- *Engagement*
- *Relationships*
- *Meaning*
- *Accomplishments*

The Children's Hope Scale measures (a) agency (goal-directed energy) and (b) pathways (planning to meet goals) and found that hope is highly, positively related to better academic performance, reduced anxiety and self-deprecatory thinking in academic situations, and a positive problem-solving orientation.

The VIA Youth Survey is an online assessment of a person's 24 character strengths, organized into six overarching virtues:

- Wisdom
- Courage
- Humanity
- Justice
- Temperance
- Transcendence

The VIA character strengths include such areas as creativity, honesty, kindness, bravery, social intelligence, teamwork, fairness, leadership, humility, gratitude, and hope, all organized under the six virtues.

There are a number of measures associated with SDT that provide information on students' perceptions of choice, autonomy, agency, and engagement.

The Self-Determination Inventory: Student Report is a freely available standardized measure of self-determination constructed from Causal Agency Theory.

Technology is critical to changing the educational paradigm. Instead of using technology to offer prescribed and predetermined teaching to students, in self-determined education, the ownership of technology in schools is returned to the children. The child, instead of the teacher, determines when and how to use technology to learn, as well as what to learn.

The ownership of technology can only be returned to children when the ownership of learning is returned to them. In other words, when children own their learning, they can determine how to use technology to support their learning.

Technology can be used for:

- *Inquiry*. Children can use technology to find answers to their questions.

- *Collaboration.* Children can use technology to seek peer collaborators and partners in learning beyond their immediate physical environment.
- *Creation.* Children can use technology to access expertise and peers from a distance to pursue their unique and to develop creativity and entrepreneurial spirit through creating authentic products and services that are of value to others.
- *Assessment and organization.* Children can use technology to organize, manage, assess, and present their self-determined learning experiences.

Educators need to help children develop digital competency—capacities to live productively and healthily in the digital world—and avoid the dark side of technology.

Self-Determined
Education for All

"Schools everywhere could initiate an Independent Project," wrote Engel (2011) in her *New York Times* op-ed piece. "All it takes are serious, committed students and a supportive faculty."

Engel is right. The Independent Project, discussed in Chapter 1, appears to be an easy way to model how to implement self-determined education. First, the Independent Project was not a complete overhaul of the existing school. It did not attempt to force everyone to adopt the new paradigm. It did not disrupt the entire school. Instead, it was an alternative for a small number of students who chose to experience a new approach. It was an invitation rather than an imposition. As a result, it was not rejected, although it did meet with some resistance. This school-within-a-school approach has a better chance to succeed than a wholesale approach that attempts to make changes to the entire school, especially a public school that is deeply entangled with federal and state regulations and requirements, as discussed in Chapter 4.

Second, the Independent Project was homegrown. It was not a ready-made program created by someone outside the school, nor were there any outside consultants. It naturally evolved with the people inside the school community. This approach reduced the kind of resistance, rejection, and skepticism that often accompanies outside products.

Third, the Independent Project did not add substantial extra financial costs to the school. Although it did take the staff time of the faculty advisers, teaching these students in regular courses required staff time anyway. It apparently did not require significant investment in extra staffing. The project did not require extra facilities or equipment either. Thus, it should be easier for budget-conscious schools to adopt the program.

David Lane's Experiment

David Lane put Engel's belief to the test at Leominster High School (LHS), located just about 100 miles east of Monument Mountain Regional High School, the birthplace of the Independent Project. Lane, a teacher at LHS, has been trying to implement the Independent Project for more than five years, since around March 2013, when he watched the viral YouTube video about the Independent Project at the suggestion of a student.

That student and a group of other students in his speech class decided that they should try to start a similar program at their high school. Lane, a veteran teacher and a long-time believer of self-directed education, endorsed the decision and began the bumpy and emotional journey. Lane recounted his journey in a four-part essay series published in 2018.

To start, Lane and his students wrote a proposal and delivered it to the school principal. The principal was cautious but receptive. He suggested changing the program from a full-day school-within-a-school model to one period a day so they could offer it in the following academic year (since it was too late to get approval for the full-day program like the original Independent Project). The principal promised to present the proposal to the school committee and request expanding it the following year if the program was shown to benefit students.

Lane agreed to lead the modified Independent Project class in the 2013–2014 school year. The pilot program was apparently a success—at least not a disaster—as "students learned Japanese, created artwork, studied comparative religion, analyzed literature, explored healthy diets, and researched statistics," according to Lane, who added, "these students, by the way, have gone on to careers in linguistics, photography, education, sports management, and health care." Another piece of evidence of success is that the principal did not ask Lane to stop the program. Instead, he supported its possible expansion to a full-day program and offered to put the Independent Project into Lane's schedule as a regular class. Lane was leading the class on top of his full teaching schedule during the pilot year.

However, the arrival of a new superintendent in the district disrupted the plan to expand the program as originally designed. The principal asked Lane to wait one more year for expansion. So the program was offered as one period in the day for the 2014–2015 school year.

More disruption would come. The new superintendent and Lane's high school principal did not agree on the direction of the school. The principal resigned and left the district. Although the principal did make sure that program was still in the schedule and would continue in 2015–2016, the promised and expected expansion plan was put on hold amid the uncertainty about the school's future leadership. Lane and the students "could not help but feel betrayed" (Lane, 2018).

And it got worse. The interim principal canceled the program. She apparently made the decision unilaterally, "without ever visiting the class or speaking with me or the students in the program," wrote Lane. "She didn't even inform me of her decision" (Lane, 2018). After finding out that the Independent Project was not on his schedule for the following year, Lane was infuriated. "I almost resigned that day" (Lane, 2018).

Lane found new hope in the hiring of a permanent principal. He strategically asked the students in the project to meet with the principal during his visit to the school before he officially came on board. Apparently, the students did an excellent job selling the project. "Fifteen minutes later, he walked into my classroom with the kids," recounts Lane. "He immediately became a fan of our program."

The new principal reinstated the program during the second semester, which started in January 2016. But the program was still only offered for one period a day. The following year, the program was expanded to two sections, but still for only one period a day.

Lane did not give up his dream to run the program as it was originally conceived. With the backing and encouragement of his new principal, he developed a proposal for the district's school committee to open the Independent Project as a full-day program. But it was too late to be considered when the proposal was ready in April 2017 because decisions about study programs had already been made for the following year.

"I was crushed," writes Lane. But he was encouraged by the principal not to give up. The Independent Project was getting more popular, too. Ninety students requested to be part of the program in the 2017–2018 school year. The principal told Lane that he could spend most of his time teaching the project, as it expanded to three sections. But it remained only one period a day.

Lane still wanted a full-day program owned by students. He continued to promote the proposal. The superintendent told him that he liked the proposal, and he would deliver it to the district's school committee for consideration. He also promised to include Lane on the agenda of the next committee meeting so Lane could make his case for the program. But that promise was not fulfilled. The superintendent "quit and walked off the job before the end of his contract and before our proposal was placed on the agenda" (Lane, 2018).

An interim superintendent came on board in December 2017. Lane emailed her to inform her of the promise of her predecessor and told her that he was eager to present the proposal at the school committee's next meeting. He received no response from the interim superintendent directly. Instead, she had instructed the high school principal to inform Lane that his proposal would not be included on the agenda of any school committee meetings that year. The superintendent told the principal that "with all of the upheaval in the district, it was not 'the right time' to propose a new program for the high school" (Lane, 2018).

No one else responded to Lane's proposal. No suggestions, no appreciation, not even critique was received, as if the proposal had never existed. Lane was discouraged. "It's been five years since we started. The Independent Project at our high school will not grow next year—or likely, ever" (Lane, 2018).

It did not grow. The Independent Project was eliminated. Lane resigned from LHS and left Massachusetts to become a principal of a charter school in New Hampshire in 2018.

Lane's experiment proves that Engel was right. Yes, the Independent Project was successfully implemented. At the same time, it also proves that Engel was wrong. The project was indeed initiated; however, it did not grow. It was at best a partial implementation. Instead of a whole-day school-within-a-school, the Independent Project became a class—one period a day. And this partial implementation, while easy to get started, had negative consequences.

The significance of Lane's five-year experience with promoting self-determined education goes way beyond a case to test whether the Independent Project can be replicated in any school. In many ways, Lane's experience with implementing the Independent Project is quite typical. So is the experience of the Independent Project at Monument High. The experience is consistent with research findings about implementing innovations in public education. As such, it has significant implications for future efforts to implement self-determined education in the conventional system.

In previous chapters, we have laid out the case for self-determined learning for all students. We have also described examples where self-determined learning is taking place in many schools around the world. Furthermore, we presented strategies to help students develop their capacity for self-determined learning. Additionally, we discussed the conditions necessary to enable self-determined learning. In this concluding chapter, we'll first discuss the lessons we can learn from Lane's sobering journey with the implementation of the Independent Project in his high school. We'll then attempt to provide a few practical recommendations for teachers and school leaders who are interested in making self-determined education available to all students all the time, regardless of their age and location.

Lessons from the Experiment

David Lane's experiment offers a number of important insights. Simply speaking, shifting the conventional education paradigm is much more challenging and complex than initiating a project. It requires much more than a few committed individuals.

Champions Are Necessary

Despite David Lane's frustration with the lack of expansion of the Independent Project at LHS, the fact that he was able to start the project suggests that there are devoted and informed educators who are frustrated with conventional education and are constantly looking for a better education for their students. Lane is an example; so is Mike Powell, the admissions counselor who was instrumental in initiating the original Independent Project at Monument High.

There are also numerous students who are tired of their educational experiences and are searching for something different. The student who brought the Independent Project video to the attention of Lane and Samuel Levin, who started the original project, are excellent examples, as are the students who worked with Lane and Levin to start the Independent Project at the two high schools.

Many educators and students are waiting for a champion, an instigator—someone who is willing to put forth a plan or propose an action. With his mother, Levin at Monument High was the instigator of the Independent Project there. The student who introduced the Independent Project video to Lane was an instigator with Lane.

Anyone can be a champion—a student, parent, teacher, school leader, or member of the community. But champions need to have a few qualities. First, they need to be quite dissatisfied with the current situation, otherwise there is no need for them to seek change. Lane was unhappy with conventional education, as was Levin.

Second, they need to have confidence that they can make changes. Many people may be very dissatisfied with conventional education, but few believe that they can do anything about it. Lane and Levin believed that they could initiate changes, and that makes them examples of champions.

Third, they need to have the courage to initiate the change and take responsibility for possible consequences. Many people may be dissatisfied and have confidence that they can make changes, but they may be concerned about the extra time required and, more important, potential negative consequences. Besides potential poor outcomes of the change, there are other negative consequences associated with change, such as possible conflicts with the leadership and rejection (jealousy) from colleagues. Levin and Lane demonstrated the courage by taking the initiative to implement a project to support self-determined learning.

Fourth, champions need to be alert to inspirational moments. Many people may be dissatisfied and have the confidence and courage, but they may not encounter the moment of inspiration when an idea triggers their action. The inspiration can come from any experience—reading a book, listening to a presentation, observing a class, or perhaps hiking. Moments of inspiration are often unplanned and unexpected. So, champions need to be alert and ready to act. In the case of Levin, the moment was when his mother asked the question, "Why don't you create your own school?" For Lane, it was when he watched the YouTube video about the Independent Project.

Champions Alone Are Not Enough

People with the qualities of champions exist in every school. But to succeed, they need a supportive environment. A supportive environment is hard to find.

A supportive environment is much more than a few supportive individuals. It includes the collective mindset, culture, and institutional infrastructure of a school. The support of individuals such as a school principal may be sufficient for small changes that do not challenge the existing culture or change the existing institutional arrangement. More significant and meaningful changes require institutional changes. And these changes are hard to come by in the conventional education system. As a result, it seems easy to start self-determined education, but it is difficult to sustain and expand it so that more students can have more control of more of their time.

Lane was able to initiate the Independent Project at LHS because there were a few supportive individuals, or at least individuals in leadership positions, who did not actively resist or reject the initiative. Out of the three principals experiencing the Independent Project, one was at least receptive and supportive, one was extremely supportive, and one showed resistance and canceled the program. Out of the three superintendents overlapping with the project, the first one was not aware of the project, the second one appeared to be supportive (willing to put the proposal in front of the school committee), and the third one was, at worst, unknown (no information about her view of the proposal, but she was preoccupied with other things). We don't know the views of members of the district's school committee because they may not even have read the proposal.

Although there was skepticism among the staff at LHS about the Independent Project, they did not initially reject it. Later, as class sizes grew due to a budget crisis in the district, there was growing sentiment among Lane's colleagues that the Independent Project was a waste of time and resources, according to Lane. But that sentiment was not directly responsible for the lack of growth of the project. In fact, Lane was able to convince four of his colleagues to take a trip to visit a shining example of self-determined education—North Star, an organization that practices education without schooling. There was some skepticism among the faculty at Monument High initially as well.

"Adults in the school district leadership had made a mess of things," Lane wrote in his essay. The adults' mess was the most direct cause of the delay of the expansion of the Independent Project. The personnel turmoil, budget crisis, and politics did not afford the project a chance to grow. What happened at LHS and the district in terms of the budget crisis, politics, and leadership shakeup during the five years is not that uncommon in the public education system. The system is designed by adults and serves adults. As a result, the system is more concerned about the interests of adults than those of children. The system can tolerate small changes but does not want to be bothered by efforts that distract its fight over adults' interests.

In other words, what stopped the expansion of the Independent Project at LHS was institutional inertia, a tendency to do nothing or remain unchanged. It is clear that the school and school district were not actively pushing for change. The school did not reject the project outright, but it did not proactively encourage it or enthusiastically embrace it. It sort of dealt with a committed education innovator and his eager students as an inconvenience. There was no special effort on behalf of the school to change the school committee agenda or timing of approval programs to consider the proposal. The school and school district were just carrying on its business as usual. There was no institutional mechanism for, or interest in, stimulating changes in the school district.

Dosage Matters

Due to the lack of a supportive environment, the Independent Project at LHS failed to grow. And the lack of growth proved to be detrimental to the program. Lane (2018) "was sure that continuing to run the Independent Project as a one-period-a-day class would be counterproductive" (Lane, 2018). He was right. Instead of pursuing exciting things to learn in his Independent Project class like the students did in the first year, most students in the 2017–2018 school year chose to use their time to do homework and projects for their other classes. Every student in the project spent at least one day a week choosing to do homework or projects for other classes. To honor his promise to let the students decide how to use their time, Lane did not intervene.

This was certainly not the outcome Lane expected from giving back to students the right of self-determination over their education. While some may point out that this result is proof that students are unable to truly use their time well and thus cannot be trusted to have self-determination over their education, Lane believes the real problem is the opposite: students did not have enough freedom because the freedom to make decisions about what, how, and why to learn cannot be limited to one hour a day. Students in the program cannot come from, and then go to, classes where curriculum is standardized and they are told to learn things they are not interested in "or else" and then simultaneously internalize the knowledge that no one can ever limit, restrict, or prevent them from learning whatever they want to learn. We cannot successfully convince young people that they are free to choose to use their time to learn what they want, when most of the time they simply are not (Lane, 2018).

Lane points out a crucial practical issue concerning self-determined education—the issue of dosage. In medical treatment, one must have sufficient exposure to the treatment to experience the intended effect. The exposure includes dosage each time, frequency, and the total amount of the treatment. One cannot take only half of the prescribed amount and expect the intended outcome. The same is true for educational treatment. Students must be sufficiently exposed to an education program to have the expected outcome. In the case of the Independent Project, one cannot expect students to have the same outcome when they only experience self-determination one period a day as when they are provided the opportunity to exercise self-determination for a whole day.

We advocate that students exert self-determination over their education for their entire school career. But that is too radical for many conventional schools, at least in the beginning, as demonstrated by Lane's experience. Many schools have legitimate concerns about helping students meet state standards and college admissions. So realistically, it is not possible for many schools to change their practices overnight.

As a result, we need to ask the question about threshold; that is, how much freedom is the minimum amount needed that students can reap the benefits of self-determination? If one period is not sufficient, would two periods a day or a half day work? And if it is determined that a school cannot offer the minimum, should they not even try? Or is something better than nothing?

A related question is whether one semester is sufficient. The original Independent Project ran for one semester. It is apparent that this one semester produced significant outcomes. But what if the students had one semester for two years, three years, or an entire year? Would they have achieved a lot more?

There is no right answer to these questions because the answer is largely determined by the expected outcomes and also the quality of the program. There is no systematic empirical research that suggests what amount is right, either. However, Lane's advice is not to start the program as one-period-a-day course.

Students Surrender Their Right to Self-Determination

"No one can take away a person's right to learn what, how, and why to learn, but a person can surrender it," Lane concludes upon reflection over the fact that many of the students in his Independent Project chose to use the freedom to do homework and work from other courses. He laments (2018):

> But think about that. When given the freedom to choose HOW to use their own time, almost all of them, at least sometimes, chose to do work they do NOT want to do, work they are doing because others force them to do it.

There are many reasons for students to surrender their right to self-determination. It is a practical way to gain more time that they can have control over. As Lane observed, some of the students wanted to use the Independent Project time to do school work so they could have more time after school to pursue their own interests. In other words, the students wanted control of their own time, but they accepted schooling as a necessary evil they had to deal with. So if they could use school time to do school work, they were happy to take that option.

Students have been conditioned not to believe that they have the right to determine what to learn, when to learn, or how to learn. The moment they start school, most students are taught to follow a uniform standardized curriculum. They are rarely given the opportunity to choose what they want to learn, let alone asked what they want to learn. As a result, most students have never had the experience of making decisions about what they learn in schools.

Likewise, students' time is structured in school to the minute. They follow a premade uniform schedule. They are not allowed to be late for class (let alone miss one) even when they are engaged in more meaningful educational activities (such as having an important conversation with schoolmates, completing an art project, or reading an engaging book). To be a good student, one has to be on time for every class.

In a similar fashion, students are given little choice over how they learn. They must follow the teacher, who has, in turn, been trained to deliver lessons in certain ways. They must obtain information from resources chosen by adults. They must also carry out the activities the teacher prescribes in the class. Moreover, they must demonstrate their learning in ways and through actions their teacher deems acceptable.

Conventional schooling rewards compliance and punishes disobedience. The system uses grades and test scores to sort students to allocate resources. Compliant students earn better grades and higher test scores, so they are recognized as good students. Good students are celebrated and given the opportunities to go to better colleges. Better colleges lead to higher social status and a better income, although it has been found that degrees have little to do with actual job performance (Frankiewicz, 2019). In the meantime, so-called noncompliant students are considered poor or bad students and deprived of a decent future. As a result, most students have come to accept that unless they do what schools want them to do, their futures are doomed. Thus, taking control of their own learning is uncomfortable and scary to many students.

Furthermore, students need to learn how to best use their time productively. When students are not given the opportunity to learn how to make sound decisions about learning and the skills to manage their own learning, they do not develop the skills and knowledge needed for exercising self-determination. As a result, when they are suddenly given the freedom, they are at a loss and easily retreat to what they know and are comfortable with.

It is, therefore, not surprising to see students surrender their right to self-determination over their education. Even when the right is returned to them, as Lane did in his Independent Project class, many students reject the objective truth that they can have control over their own learning. Lane (2018) recounts his observations:

> Presenting young people with the objective truth that they are always in control of their own time is sometimes as far as I get. I am not sure it is enough, but in the Independent Project, it is undeniable. It puts them in a position where they must confront the power they have within themselves, the control they have over the quality of their own time. Many of my students reject this truth, though. It is too much for them.

What Can We (You) Do

Since you have come so far with this book, you must be convinced of the need to make self-determined education available for all children. If so, the lessons from Lane's journey point to a number of actions that we (you) can all take to make that happen, regardless of our (your) role in education today.

Students

Students are perhaps the most powerful agents in leading the change. Schools exist because of students. Without students, schools disappear. Thus, students can exert the most pressure on the conventional education system and institutions.

We hope all students recognize this fact, refuse to be defined by schooling, and actively demand the return of their right to self-determined education. As students, you should refuse to be defined by schools. Your grades do not define who you are or can be; neither do your test scores. If you are dissatisfied with your education experience, take action and create a different one, like Levin and the student who brought the Independent Project video to the attention of Lane.

Students can do more, beyond affecting their own learning. They can achieve a much broader impact on education. Nikhil Goyal, for example, was so unhappy with the education system that he wrote the powerful book, *One Size Does Not Fit All: A Student's Assessment of School* (2012) when he was in high school. He did not go to college and became an influential journalist and writer on education. He published another book in 2016, *Schools on Trial: How Freedom and Creativity Can Fix Our Educational Malpractice*. Sydney Smooth, a 4th grader, delivered a two-minute speech about standardized testing to members of the Hernando County School Board in Florida in 2015. In her speech, she complained that "testing looks at me as a number" and "[o]ne test defines me as either a failure or a success through a numbered rubric." A video of her speech went viral and had over two million views as of January 2019. Levin also authored a book with his mother, Engel, to share his experiences creating the Independent Project (2016).

Teachers

Teachers are the primary actors in the conventional education system. They are the most visible element of education to students. The impact of the conventional education system is delivered to students through teachers. Thus, they have the most influence over students' daily experiences. Teachers can help students experience self-determined education in a number of ways.

Respect students' rights. The least a teacher can do is to respect a student's right to self-determined learning. We understand that teachers in conventional education are under pressure to execute the will of the system and deliver prescribed content. They are held accountable for their students' academic performance. But when encountered with students who do not benefit from conventional schooling and want to pursue their own learning, teachers should at least allow them to do so without punishing or alienating them.

Be a partner. Teachers can do more. They can help students who wish to exercise self-determination over their education as partners. A teacher does not have to change the entire class to help a few individual students interested in pursuing their own learning.

Be a provider. Teachers can provide self-determination in their classes. They can turn part of, or the entirety of, their classes into student-determined education. They can also actively help students develop skills for self-determined education, as discussed in previous chapters.

Be a champion. We hope more teachers can become champions for self-determined education. Like Lane, they can advocate for students' right to self-determined education and lead the creation of programs that provide self-determined education. Furthermore, they can champion for self-determined education by spreading the word, such as conducting professional development for colleagues and promoting self-determined education to their leaders and the general public through writings and presentations at meetings.

School Leaders

Those who occupy school leadership positions are the guardians of the education system. School board members, superintendents, principals, curriculum directors, and other leadership position occupants are responsible for the institutional culture of schools. While students and teachers can indeed initiate programs, whether the programs can grow and spread is largely affected by the institutional culture, as demonstrated by Lane's experience.

School leaders can create an environment that stimulates, supports, and promotes innovations and celebrates innovative teachers and students. They can create space for innovation by relaxing regulations and standardization. They can incentivize innovations by establishing grants dedicated to supporting self-determined education programs. They can establish institutional infrastructures, such as dedicated offices, to promote self-determined education. If opportunities exist, they can actively and creatively develop programs or schools that espouse self-determined education.

Policymakers

Policymakers at various levels of the education system should begin to accept that the traditional education paradigm is outdated. The system built upon this paradigm is unable to meet the educational needs of children and society today, let alone the future. Investing in efforts to improve the system will not be sufficient. What we need is a new paradigm.

Recognizing that the new paradigm cannot be imposed on all students and all schools at once, policymakers can start by allowing and supporting grassroots innovations that afford students opportunities for self-determined education. The next step is to enact policies and programs to stimulate innovations in this area. Gradually, they should enact policies to mandate that schools offer self-determination as an option for all children. This also means to sunset policies that aim to reinforce the traditional education paradigm, such as a uniform curriculum and standardized-test-based accountability measures.

Combating Stockholm Syndrome: Final Words

Stockholm Syndrome is a psychological condition that causes hostages to develop a psychological bonding with their captors. Psychologist Frank M. Ochberg, cofounder of the National Center for Critical Incident Analysis and former associate director of the National Institute of Mental

Health, coined the term to describe the love relationship developed by a hostage toward his captor in a kidnapping case that took place in Stockholm, Sweden. It is "a primitive gratitude for the gift of life, an emotion that eventually develops and differentiates into varieties of affection and love," wrote Ochberg (2005) in a commentary published in the *Los Angeles Times*.

We in education all suffer from Stockholm Syndrome. We have all been held hostage by conventional education. We are grateful that that education has helped us become who we are. We have developed different love relationships with conventional education. We are fearful of losing or upsetting our love.

But it is time for us to reject this irrational feeling and cut our ties with conventional education. For the sake of our future, we need to start making self-determined education an option for all children!

Research to Practice: Self-Determined Education for All

Shifting the conventional education paradigm requires champions. Anyone—a student, parent, teacher, school leader, or member of the community—can be a champion. But champions need to have a few qualities. They need

- To be dissatisfied with the current situation.
- To have confidence that they can make changes.
- To have the courage to initiate the change and take responsibility for possible consequences.
- To be alert to inspirational moments.

But champions alone are not enough. To succeed, students need a supportive environment that includes the collective mindset, culture, and institutional infrastructure of a school.

Further, dosage matters. One cannot expect students to have the same outcome when they only experience student ownership and self-determination for one period a day as when they are provided the opportunity to exercise self-determination for a whole day.

Students have been conditioned to not believe that they have the right to determine what to learn, when to learn, or how to learn. The moment they start school, most students are taught to follow a uniform standardized curriculum. They are rarely given the opportunity to choose what they want to learn, let alone asked what they want to learn. As a result, most students have never had the experience of making decisions about what they learn in schools.

Students, perhaps the most powerful agents in leading the change, along with teachers, the primary actors in the conventional education system, can become a critical force in creating change.

continued

Research to Practice: Self-Determined Education for All (*continued*)

Teachers can help students experience self-determined education in a number of ways:

- Respect students' rights.
- Be a partner.
- Be a provider.
- Be a champion.

School leaders can

- Create an environment that stimulates, supports, and promotes innovations and celebrates innovative teachers and students.
- Create the space for innovation by relaxing regulations and standardization.
- Incentivize innovations by establishing grants dedicated to supporting self-determined education programs.
- Establish institutional infrastructures, such as dedicated offices, to promote self-determined education.
- If opportunities exist, actively and creatively develop programs or schools that espouse self-determined education.

Policymakers can

- Enact policies and programs to stimulate innovations in self-determined education.
- Enact policies to mandate that schools offer self-determination as an option for all children.
- Discontinue/sunset policies that aim to reinforce the traditional education paradigm, such as uniform curriculum and standardized-test-based accountability measures.

We need to start making self-determined education an option for all children.

Bibliography

Abeles, V. (Director, Producer). (2015). *Beyond measure: The revolution starts now* [Film]. Reel Link Films.

Alperovitz, G. (2005). *America beyond capitalism: Reclaiming our wealth, our liberty, and our democracy*. Hoboken,NJ: John Wiley & Sons.

Angyal, A. (1941). *Foundations for a science of personality*. Cambridge, MA: Harvard University Press.

Apple, M. W., & Beane, J. A. (1995). *Democratic schools*. Alexandria, VA: ASCD.

Australian Curriculum Assessment and Reporting Authority. (2010). *A curriculum for all young Australians*. Retrieved from http://www.acara.edu.au/verve/_resources/Information_Sheet_A_curriculum_for_all_young_Australians.pdf

Bailey, M. J., & Dynaski, S. M. (2011). Inequality in postsecondary education. In G. J. Duncan & R. J. Murnane (Eds.), *Whither opportunity? Rising inequality, schools, and children's life chances* (pp. 117–132). New York/Chicago: Russell Sage Foundation/Spencer Foundation.

Becker, M. (2012). Einstein probably. Retrieved from http://www.news.hypercrit.net/2012/11/13/einstein-on-insanity/

Beghetto, R. (2018). *What if? Building students' problem-solving skills through complex challenges*. Alexandria,VA: ASCD.

Benjamin, C. (1996). *Problem solving in school*. Upper Saddle River, NJ: Globe Fearon Educational Publisher.

Beyth-Marom, R., Fischhoff, B., Jacobs Quadrel, M., & Furby, L. (1991). Teaching decision making to adolescents: A critical review. In J. Baron & R.V. Brown (Eds.), *Teaching decision making to adolescents*. Hillsdale, NJ: Lawrence Erlbaum Associates.

Birnbaum, R. (2004). The end of shared governance: Looking ahead or looking back. *New directions for higher education, 2004*(127), 5–22.

Blasi, J. R., Freeman, R. B., & Kruse, D. (2014). *The citizen's share:Reducing inequality in the 21st century* (Paperback ed.). New Haven, CT: Yale University Press.

Bonk, C. J., Lee, M. M., Reeves, T. C., & Reynolds, T. H. (Eds.). (2015). *MOOCs and open education around the world*. New York: Routledge.

Botti, S., & McGill, A. L. (2006). When choosing is not deciding: The effect of perceived responsibility on satisfaction. *Journal of Consumer Research, 33*(2), 211–219.

Broudy, H. S. (1982). What knowledge is of most worth? *Educational Leadership, May*, 574–578.

Brunello, G., & Schlotter, M. (2010). *The effect of noncognitive skills and personality traits on labour market outcomes*. Retrieved from http://www.epis.pt/downloads/dest_15_10_2010.pdf

Brynjolfsson, E., & McAfee, A. (2014). *The second machine age: Work, progress, and prosperity in a time of brilliant technologies* (1st ed.). New York: W. W. Norton & Company.

Bundick, M. J. (2011). Extracurricular activities, positive youth development, and the role of meaningfulness of engagement. *The Journal of Positive Psychology, 6*(1), 57–74.

Byrnes, J. P. (2002). *The nature and development of decision making: A self-regulation model*. Mahwah, NJ: Lawrence Erlbaum Associates.

Byun, S.-Y., & Kim, K.-K. (2010). Educational inequality in South Korea: The widening socioeconomic gap in student achievement. *Research in Sociology of Education, 17*, 155–182.

Cadwalladr, C. (2015, August 02). The "granny cloud": The network of volunteers helping poorer children learn. *The Guardian*. Retrieved from https://www.theguardian.com/education/2015/aug/02/sugata-mitra-school-in-the-cloud

CAST. (2018). *Universal design for learning guidelines version 2.2* [graphic organizer]. Wakefield, MA: Author. Retrieved from http://udlguidelines.cast.org/more/about-graphic-organizer

Chamberlin, R. (2016). *Free children and democratic schools: A philosophical study of liberty and education*. New York: Routledge.

Chen, M. (2014, June 17). Student Power! Retrieved from ttps://www.edutopia.org/blog/student-power-milton-chen

Clark, L. (2016). *Beautiful failures: How the quest for success is harming our kids*. Sydney, Australia: Penguin Random House Australia.

Colorado Education Initiative. (n.d.). *Grade 9–12 decision making*. Retrieved from http://www.coloradoedinitiative.org/wp-content/uploads/2014/10/Grade-HS-Decision-Making.pdf

Common Core State Standards Initiative. (2011). Home page. Retrieved from http://http://www.corestandards.org/

Costa, A. L. L., & Kallick, B. (2013). *Dispositions: Reframing teaching and learning*. Thousand Oaks, CA: Corwin Press.

Csikszentmihalyi, M. (1991). *Flow: The psychology of optimal experience*. New York: HarperCollins.

Cuban, L. (1986). *Teachers and machines: The classroom uses of technology since 1920*. New York: Teachers College Press.

Cuban, L. (1993). Computers meet classroom: Classroom wins. *Teachers College Record, 95*(2), 185–210.

Cuban, L. (2001). *Oversold and underused: Computers in schools 1980–2000*. Cambridge, MA: Harvard University Press.

Cuban, L. (2004). The open classroom. *Education Next, 4*(2). Retrieved from https://www.educationnext.org/theopenclassroom/

Damon, W. (2008). *The path to purpose: How young people find their calling in life*. New York: Free Press.

Darling-Hammond, L. (2010). *The flat world and education: How America's commitment to equity will determine our future*. New York: Teachers College Press.

Deci, E. L., Hodges, R., Pierson, L., & Tomassone, J. (1992). Autonomy and competence as motivational factors in students with learning disabilities and emotional handicaps. *Journal of Learning Disabilities, 25*(7), 457–471.

Deci, E. L., & Ryan, R. M. (2012). Motivation, personality, and development within embedded social contexts: An overview of self-determination theory. In R. M. Ryan (Ed.), *The Oxford handbook of human motivation* (pp. 85–110). Oxford: Oxford University Press.

Deci, E. L., & Ryan, R. M. (2016). Optimizing students' motivation in the era of testing and pressures: A self-determination theory perspective. In W. C. Liu, J. C. K. Wang, & R. M. Ryan (Eds.), *Building autonomous learners: Perspectives from research and practice using self-determination theory* (pp. 9–29). New York: Springer.

Deci, E. L., Ryan, R. M., & Guay, F. (2013). Self-determination theory and actualization of human potentials. In D. M. McInerney, H. W. Marsh, R. G. Craven, F. Guay (Eds.), *Theory driving research: New wave perspectives on self-processes and human development* (pp. 109–133). Charlotte, NC: Information Age Publishing.

De Roo, G. (2017). *Environmental planning in the Netherlands: Too good to be true: From command-and-control planning to shared governance*. New York: Routledge.

Dewey, J. (1938). *Experience and Education*. New York: Collier Books.

Dewey, J. (1975). *Democracy and education: An introduction to the philosophy of education*. New York: Free Press.

Dominguez, P. R., Gamiz, F., Gil, M., Moreno, H., Zamora, R. M., Gallo, M., … de Brugada, I. (2013). Providing choice increases children's vegetable intake. *Food Quality and Preference, 30*(2), 109–113.

Duckworth, A. L., & Yeager, D. S. (2015). Measurement matters: Assessing personal qualities other than cognitive ability for educational purposes. *Educational Researcher, 44*(4), 237–251.

Duncan, G. J., & Murnane, R. J. (Eds.). (2011). *Whither opportunity? Rising inequality, schools, and children's life chances*. New York/Chicago: Russell Sage Foundation/Spencer Foundation.

Dweck, C. S. (2008). *Mindset: The new psychology of success*. New York: Ballantine Books.

D'Zurilla, T. J., Nezu, A. M., & Maydeu-Olivares, A. (2004). Social problem solving: Theory and assessment. In E. C. Chang, T. J. D'Zurilla, & L. J. Sanna (Eds.). *Social problem solving: Theory, research, and training*. Washington, DC: American Psychological Association.

Ellenberg, J. (2014). *How not to be wrong: The power of mathematical thinking*. New York: Penguin Press.

Engel, S. (2011, March 15). Let kids rule the school. *The New York Times*. Retrieved from https://www.nytimes.com/2011/03/15/opinion/15engel.html?_r=0

European Communities. (2006). *Key competences for lifelong learning: A European framework*. Retrieved from https://eur-lex.europa.eu/legal-content/EN/TXT/?uri=uriserv%3AOJ.C_.2018.189.01.0001.01.ENG&toc=OJ%3AC%3A2018%3A189%3ATOC

The European Parliament, & The Council of the European Union. (2006, December 12). *Recommendation of the European Parliament and of the Council of the European Union on key competences for lifelong learning.* Retrieved from http://eur-lex.europa.eu/LexUriServ/site/en/oj/2006/l_394/l_39420061230en00100018 .pdf

Executive Office of the President. (2016). *Artificial intelligence, automation, and the economy.* Retrieved from https://obamawhitehouse.archives.gov/sites/whitehouse.gov/files/documents/Artificial-Intelligence -Automation-Economy.PDF

Feldman, D. L., Smith, A. T., & Waxman, B. L. (2017). *Why we drop out: Understanding and disrupting student pathways to leaving school.* New York: Teachers College Press.

Florida, R. (2012). *The rise of the creative class: Revisited* (2nd ed.). New York: Basic Books.

Ford, D. Y., & Grantham, T. C. (2003). Providing access for culturally diverse gifted students: From deficit to dynamic thinking. *Theory into Practice, 42*(3), 217–225.

Frankiewicz, T. C.-P. (2019, January 7). Does higher education still prepare people for jobs? *Harvard Business Review, January 07,* Online. Retrieved from https://hbr.org/2019/2001/does-higher-education -stillprepare-people-for-jobs

Fryer, R. G., & Levitt, S. D. (2004). Understanding the black-white test score gap in the first two years of school. *The Review of Economics and Statistics, 86*(2), 447–464.

Gallup. (2004). Most teens associate school with boredom, fatigue. Retrieved from https://news. gallup .com/poll/11893/most-teens-associate-school-boredom-fatigue.aspx

Gallup. (2017). Gallup Student Poll: Engaged today—Ready for tomorrow. Retrieved from http://www. gallup.com/file/education/233681/2017 GSP Scorecard. pdf?g_source=link_wwwv9&g_campaign =item_233555&g_medium=copy

Gardner, H. (1983). *Frames of mind: The theory of multiple intelligences.* New York: Basic Books.

Gardner, H. (2007). *Five minds for the future.* Boston: Harvard Business School Press.

Geelong Grammar School. (2016). *School performance information 2016.* Victoria, AU: Author. Retrieved from file:///C:/Users/mlw/Downloads/School%20Performance%20Information%202014.pdf

Gillet, N., Vallerand, R. J., & Lafrenière, M. K. (2012). Intrinsic and extrinsic school motivation as a function of age: The mediating role of autonomy support. *Social Psychology of Education, 15*(1), 77–95.

Gleason, D. L. (2017). *At what cost? Defending adolescent development in fiercely competitive schools.* Raleigh, NC: Lulu Press.

Goldin, C., & Katz, L. F. (2008). *The race between education and technology.* Cambridge, MA: Harvard University Press.

Goss, P., & Sonnemann, J. (2017). Engaging students: Creating classrooms that improve learning. Retrieved from https://grattan.edu.au/report/engaging-students-creating-classrooms-that-improve-learning/

Goyal, N. (2012). *One size does not fit all: A student's assessment of school.* New York: Alternative Education Resource Organization.

Goyal, N. (2016). *Schools on trial: How freedom and creativity can fix our educational malpractice.* New York: Doubleday.

Greenberg, D., Sadofsky, M., & Lempka, J. (2005). *The pursuit of happiness: The lives of Sudbury Valley alumni.* Framingham, MA: Sudbury School Press.

Guay, F., Lessard, V., & Dubois, P. (2016). How can we create better learning contexts for children? In Liu, W. C., Wang, J. C. K., & Ryan, R. M. (Eds.), *Building autonomous learners: Perspectives from research and practice using self-determination theory* (pp. 83–106). Singapore: Springer.

Hahn, J. D. (2018). Kindergarten class's morning handshake ritual has helped one nonverbal student find his voice. Retrieved from https://people.com/human-interest/kindergarten-class-morning-handshake -keene-elementary/

Hairon, S., & Goh, J. W. (2015). Pursuing the elusive construct of distributed leadership: Is the search over? *Educational Management Administration & Leadership, 43*(5), 693–718.

Hansen, M., Levesque, E. M., Quintero, D., & Valant, J. (2018, April 17). Have we made progress on achievement gaps? Looking at evidence from the new NAEP results. Retrieved from https://www .brookings.edu/blog/brown-center-chalkboard/2018/04/17/have-we-made-progress-on -achievementgaps-looking-at-evidence-from-the-new-naep-results/

Harel, I., & Papert, S. (1991). *Constructionism.* New York: Ablex Publishing.

Harris, A. (2013). *Distributed school leadership: Developing tomorrow's leaders.* New York: Routledge.

Harris, A., Leithwood, K., Day, C., Sammons, P., & Hopkins, D. (2007). Distributed leadership and organizational change: Reviewing the evidence. *Journal of Educational Change, 8*(4), 337–347.

Harris, K. R., & Graham, S. (1992). Self-regulated strategy development: A part of the writing process. In M. Pressley, K. R. Harris, & J. T. Guthrie (Eds.), *Promoting academic competence and literacy in school* (pp. 277–309). San Diego, CA: Academic Press.

Hays (2015). *Labour market in a world of continuous change: Hays Global Skills Index 2015*. Retrieved from https://www.hays-index.com/wp-content/uploads/2015/09/Hays-GSI-Report_-2015.pdf

Hofer, J., & Busch, H. (2011). Satisfying one's needs for competence and relatedness: Consequent domain-specific well-being depends on strength of implicit motives. *Personality and Social Psychology Bulletin, 37*(9), 1147–1158.

Individuals with Disabilities Education Act (IDEA). (2004).

Internet World Stats. (2019, June 30, 2018). Internet usage statistics: The internet big picture: World internet users and 2019 population stats.. Retrieved from http://www.internetworldstats.com/stats.htm

Jason, Z. (2017). Bored out of their minds. *Harvard Ed. Magazine*, Winter 2017. Retrieved from https://www.gse.harvard.edu/news/ed/17/01/bored-out-their-minds

John, O. P., Robins, R. W., & Pervin, L. A. (2008). *Handbook of personality: Theory and research* (3rd ed.). New York: Guilford Press.

Joyce, B., & Weil, M. (1980). *Models of teaching* (2nd ed.). Englewood Cliffs, NJ: Prentice Hall.

Kafai, Y. B., & Resnick, M. (Eds.). (1996). *Constructionism in practice: Designing, thinking, and learning in a digital world*. London: Routledge.

Kelly, M., Dubb, S., & Duncan, V. (2016). Broad-based ownership models as tools for job creation and community development: A guide to how community development is using broad-based ownership models to help low- and moderate-income communities. Retrieved from http://democracycollaborative.org/content/ broad-based-ownership-models-tools-job-creation-and-community-development

Kelly Services. (2009). *Kelly global workforce survey*. Retrieved from http://ir.kellyservices.com/news-releases/news-release-details/according-new-international-workplace-survey-kelly-services

Kern, M. L., Benson, L., Steinberg, E. A., & Steinberg, L. (2015). *The EPOCH measure of adolescent well-being*. Melbourne: Author. Retrieved from http://www.peggykern.org/uploads/5/6/6/7/56678211/epoch_measure_of_adolescent_well-being_102014.pdf

Knowles, M. S. (1975). *Self-directed learning: A guide for learners and teachers*. Chicago: Follett Publishing.

Krulik, S., & Rudnick, J. A. (1995). *The new sourcebook for teaching reasoning and problem solving in elementary school*. Boston: Allyn & Bacon.

Lane, D. (2018). Deschooling in school: Part 3. Retrieved from https://www.self-directed.org/tp/deschooling-in-school-3/

Laski, E. V., Jor'dan, J. R., Daoust, C., & Murray, A. K. (2015). What makes mathematics manipulatives effective? Lessons from cognitive science and Montessori education. *SAGE Open, 5*(2). doi:10.1177/2158244015589588

Leighninger, M. (2006). *The next form of democracy: How expert rule is giving way to shared governance—and why politics will never be the same*. Nashville, TN: Vanderbilt University Press.

Levin, H. M. (2012). More than just test scores. *Prospects: The Quarterly Review of Comparative Education, 42*(3), 269–284.

Levin, S., & Engel, S. (2016). *A school of our own: The story of the first student-run high school and a new vision for American education*. New York: The New Press.

Mann, L., Harmoni, R., & Power, C. (1989). Adolescent decision making: The development of competence. *Journal of Adolescence, 12*(3), 265–278.

Mann, L., Harmoni, R., Power, C., Beswick, G., & Ormand, C. (1989). Effectiveness of the GOFER course in decision making for high school students. *Journal of Behavioral Decision Making, 1*(3), 159–168.

Marques, S. C., & Lopez, S. J. (2017). The development of hope. In M. L. Wehmeyer, K. A. Shogren, T. D. Little, & S. J. Lopez (Eds.), *Development of self-determination through the life-course* (pp. 271–281). New York: Springer.

Martela, F., & Ryan, R. M. (2015). The benefits of benevolence: Basic psychological needs, beneficence, and the enhancement of well-being. *Journal of Personality, 84*(6), 750–764.

Mathewson, T. G. (2018). Using creative classroom design to promote instructional innovation. *The Hechinger Report*, April 4, 2018. Retrieved from https://hechingerreport.org/using-creative-classroom-design-to-promote-instructional-innovation/

Miller, G. A., Galanter, E., & Pribram, K. H. (1960). *Plans and the structure of behavior*. New York: Holt, Rinehart, and Winston.

Mithaug, D. E. (1993). *Self-regulation theory: How optimal adjustment maximizes gain*. Westport, CT: Praeger.

Mithaug, D. E., Mithaug, D. K., Agran, M., Martin, J. E., & Wehmeyer, M. L. (2003). *Self-determined learning theory: Construction, verification, and evaluation*. Mahwah, NJ: Lawrence Erlbaum Associates.

Mitra, S. (2007, July 17). Kids can teach themselves. Retrieved from https://www.ted.com/talks/sugata_mitra_shows_how_kids_teach_themselves

Mitra, S. (2012a). *Beyond the hole in the wall: Discover the power of self-organized learning*. Retrieved from https://www.amazon.com/Beyond-Hole-Wall-Discover-Self-Organized-ebook/dp/B0070YZSFQ/ref=la_B001KCZLKQ_1_1?s=books&ie=UTF8&qid=1500419170&sr=1-1

Mitra, S. (2012b, February 3). *The hole in the wall project and the power of self-organized learning*. Retrieved from https://www.amazon.com/dp/B0070YZSFQ/ref=cm_sw_em_r_mt_dp_U_RHfqEbMJDZN5Z

Montenegro, A. (2017). Understanding the concept of student agentic engagement for learning. *Columbian Applied Linguistics Journal, 19*(1), 117–128.

Neil, A. S. (1960). *Summerhill: A radical approach to child rearing*. Oxford: Hart Publishing.

Nezu, A. M., & D'Zurilla, T. J. (1981). Effects of problem definition and formulation on decision making in the social problem-solving process. *Behavior Therapy, 12*(1), 100–106.

Niemiec, C. P., & Ryan, R. M. (2009). Autonomy, competence, and relatedness in the classroom: Applying self-determination theory to educational practice. *Theory and Research in Education, 7*(2), 133–144.

Niemiec, R. M. (2017). *Character strengths interventions: A field guide for practitioners*. Boston: Hogrefe.

No Child Left Behind Act of 2001, P.L. 107-110, 20 U.S. C. § 6319 (2002).

Norrish, J. (2015). *Positive education: The Geelong Grammar School journey*. Oxford: Oxford University Press.

Ochberg, F. M. (2005, April 8). The ties that bind captive to captor. *Los Angeles Times*. Retrieved from http://articles.latimes.com/2005/apr/08/opinion/oe-ochberg8

OECD. (2016). *PISA 2015 results (Volume I): Excellence and equity in education*. Retrieved from: http://dx.doi.org/10.1787/9789264266490-en

OECD. (2017). *PISA 2015 results: Students' well-being*. Retrieved from http://www.keepeek.com/Digital-Asset-Management/oecd/education/pisa-2015-results-volume-iii_9789264273856-en-.Wk1WGrQ-fOQ#page1

Papert, S. (1993). *The children's machine: Rethinking school in the age of the computer*. New York: Basic Books.

Papert, S. (1999). Technology in schools—To support the system or render it obsolete? *Milken Exchange*. Retrieved from http://www.milkenexchange.org/feature/papert.html

Pappano, L. (2012, November 2). *The year of the MOOC*. Retrieved from http://www.nytimes.com/2012/11/04/education/edlife/massive-open-online-courses-are-multiplying-at-a-rapid-pace.html?pagewanted=all

Partnership for 21st Century Skills. (2007). Framework for 21st century learning. Retrieved from https://www.battelleforkids.org/networks/p21/frameworks-resources

Patall, E. A., & Hooper, S. Y (2018). The role of choice in understanding adolescent autonomy and academic functioning. In B. Soenens, M. Vansteenkiste, & S. Van Petegem (Eds.), *Autonomy in adolescent development: Toward conceptual clarity* (pp. 145–167). London: Routledge.

Peterson, C., & Seligman, M. E. P. (2004). *Character strengths and virtues: A classification and handbook*. New York and Washington, DC: Oxford University Press and American Psychological Association.

Pink, D. H. (2006). *A whole new mind: Why right-brainers will rule the future*. New York: Riverhead.

Plucker, J. A., Hardesty, J., & Burroughs, N. (2013). *Talents on the sidelines: Excellence gaps and America's persistent talent underclass*. Retrieved from https://www.researchgate.net/publication/304046990_Talent_on_the_sidelines_Excellence_gaps_and_America's_persistent_talent_underclass

Posner, R. (2009). *Lives of passion, school of hope: How one public school ignites a lifelong love of learning*. Boulder, CO: Sentient Publications.

Potter, M. (2017). Governance of higher education: Global perspectives, theories, and practices by Ian Austin and Glen A. Jones. *The Review of Higher Education, 41*(1), 141–143.

Raley, S. K., Shogren, K. A., & McDonald, A. (2018). How to implement the self-determined learning model of instruction in inclusive general education classrooms. *Teaching Exceptional Children, 51*(1), 62–71.

Rath, T., & Clifton, D. O. (2004). *How full is your bucket?* Washington, DC. Gallup Press.

Reardon, S. F. (2011). The widening academic achievement gap between the rich and the poor: New evidence and possible explanations. In G. J. Duncan & R. J. Murnane (Eds.), *Whither opportunity? Rising inequality, schools, and children's life chances* (pp. 91–116). New York/Chicago: Russell Sage Foundation/Spencer Foundation.

Redford, K. (2018). First person: When it comes to universal design for learning, don't wait to be an expert. *Education Week Teacher*, January 24, 2018. Retrieved from ttps://www.edweek.org/tm/articles/2018/01/24/when-it-comes-to-universal-design-for.html

Reeve, J. (2002). Self-determination theory applied to educational settings. In E. L. Deci & R. M. Ryan (Eds.), *Handbook of Self-Determination Research* (pp. 183–203). Rochester, NY: Rochester University Press.

Reeve, J. (2013). How students create motivationally supportive learning environments for themselves: The concept of agentic engagement. *Journal of Educational Psychology, 105*(3), 579–595.

Reeve, J., Ryan, R., Deci, E. L., & Jang, H. (2012). Understanding and promoting autonomous self-regulation: A self-determination theory perspective. In D. H. Schunk & B. J. Zimmerman (Eds.), *Motivation and self-regulated learning: Theory, research, and applications* (pp. 223–244). New York: Routledge.

Reeve, J., & Tseng, C-M. (2011). Agency as a fourth aspect of students' engagement during learning activities. *Contemporary Educational Psychology, 36*(4), 257–267.

Reimers, F. (2009). Educating for global competency. In J. E. Cohen & M. B. Malin (Eds.), *International Perspective on the Goals of Universal Basic and Secondary Education* (pp. 183–202). New York: Routlege.

Reiss, S. (2000). *Who am I: The 16 basic desires that motivate our behavior and define our personality.* New York: Jeremy P. Tarcher/Putnam.

Resnick, M. (2017). *Lifelong kindergarten: Cultivating creativity through projects, passion, peers, and play.* Cambridge, MA: The MIT Press.

Rose, T. (2016). *The end of average: How we succeed in a world that values sameness.* New York: HarperOne.

Rousso, H. (1993). *Disabled, female, and proud: Stories of ten women with disabilities.* New York: Bergin & Garvey.

Ryan, R. M., & Connell, J. P. (1989). Perceived locus of causality and internalization: Examining reasons for acting in two domains. *Journal of Personality and Social Psychology, 57*(5), 749–761.

Ryan, R. M., & Deci, E. L. (2017). *Self-determination theory: Basic psychological needs in motivation, development, and wellness.* New York: The Guilford Press.

Schleicher, A. (2018). *World class: How to build a 21st century school system.* Paris: OECD.

Schmitz, R. (2016). Crozet Elementary pilots AVID program. *The Crozet Gazette,* October 7, 2016. Retrieved from https://www.crozetgazette.com/2016/10/07/crozet-elementary-pilots-avid-program/

Schwab, K. (2015). The fourth industrial revolution: What it means and how to respond. *Foreign Affairs, December 12.* Retrieved from https://www.foreignaffairs.com/articles/2015-12-12/fourth-industrial-revolution

Seligman, M. E. P. (2011). *Flourish: A visionary new understanding of happiness and well-being.* New York: Simon & Schuster.

Sheldon, K., & Deci, E. (1993). *The self-determination scale.* University of Rochester, Rochester, NY: Author.

Sheldon, K. M., Ryan, R. M., & Reis, H. T. (1996). What makes for a good day? Competence and autonomy in the day and in the person. *Personality and Social Psychology Bulletin, 22*(12), 1270–1279.

Shogren, K. A., Raley, S. K., Burke, K. M., & Wehmeyer, M. L. (2019). *The self-determined learning model of instruction: Teacher's guide.* Lawrence, KS: Kansas University Center on Developmental Disabilities.

Shogren, K. A., & Wehmeyer, M. L. (2017). Problem solving. In M. L. Wehmeyer, K. A. Shogren, T. D. Little, & S. J. Lopez (Eds.), *Development of self-determination through the life-course* (pp. 251–260). New York: Springer.

Shogren, K. A., Wehmeyer, M. L., Forber-Pratt, A. J., & Palmer, S. B. (2015). *VIA inventory of strengths for youth (VIA-Youth): Supplement for use when supporting youth with intellectual and developmental disabilities to complete the VIA-Youth.* Lawrence, KS: Kansas University Center on Developmental Disabilities.

Shogren, K. A., Wehmeyer, M. L., & Khamsi, S. (2017). Self-initiation and planning. In M. L. Wehmeyer, K. A. Shogren, T. D. Little, & S. J. Lopez (Eds.), *Development of self-determination through the life-course* (pp. 209–217). New York: Springer.

Shogren, K. A., Wehmeyer, M. L., & Palmer, S. B. (2017). Causal agency theory. In M. L. Wehmeyer, K. A. Shogren, T. D. Little, & S. J. Lopez (Eds.), *Development of self-determination through the life-course* (pp. 55–67). New York: Springer.

Shogren, K. A., Wehmeyer, M. L., Palmer, S. B., Forber-Pratt, A., Little, T. J., & Lopez, S. J. (2017). *Self-determination inventory: Self-report.* Lawrence, KS: Kansas University Center on Developmental Disabilities.

Sifferlin, A. (2013, March 27). A high school where the students are the teachers. *Time.* Retrieved from http://healthland.time.com/2013/03/27/a-high-school-where-the-students-are-the-teachers/

Snyder, C. R., Hoza, B., Pelham, W. E., Rapoff, M., Ware, L., Danovsky, M., … Stahl, K. J. (1997). The development and validation of the children's hope scale. *Journal of Pediatric Psychology, 22*(3), 399–421.

Snyder, R. (1994). Hope and optimism. In V.S. Ramachandran (Ed.), *Encyclopedia of human behavior* (Vol. 2) (pp. 535–542). San Diego, CA: Academic Press.

Snyder, R. (2000). *Handbook of hope: Theory, measures, and applications.* San Diego, CA: Academic Press.

Snyder, R., Tran, T., Schroeder, L. L., Pulvers, K. M., Adams, V., & Laub, L. (2000). Teaching the hope recipe: Setting goals, finding pathways to those goals, and getting motivated. *Reaching Today's Youth, 4*(4), 46–50.

Soenens, B., Vansteenkiste, M., Van Petegem, S., Beyers, W., & Ryan, R. (2018). How to solve the conundrum of adolescent autonomy? On the importance of distinguishing between independence and volitional functioning. In B. Soenens, M. Vansteenkiste, & S. Van Petegem (Eds.), *Autonomy in adolescent development: Toward conceptual clarity* (pp. 1–32). London: Routledge.

Spillane, J. P. (2012). *Distributed leadership* (Vol. 4). Hoboken, NJ: John Wiley & Sons.

Spillane, J. P., Halverson, R., & Diamond, J. B. (2001). Investigating school leadership practice: A distributed perspective. *Educational Researcher, 30*(3), 23–28.

Stanford, P. (2008, January 24). Summerhill: Inside England's most controversial private school. *The Independent*. Retrieved from http://www.independent.co.uk/news/education/schools/summerhill-inside-englands-most-controversial-private-school-772976.html

Sternberg, R. J. (1988). *The triarchic mind: A new theory of human intelligence*. New York: Viking.

Sternberg, R. J., Jarvin, L., & Grigorenko, E. L. (2009). *Wisdom, intelligence, creativity, and success*. New York: Skyhorse Publishing.

The Granny Cloud. (n.d.). *Welcome to the granny cloud*. Retrieved from http://thegrannycloud.org/

Tian, M., Risku, M., & Collin, K. (2016). A meta-analysis of distributed leadership from 2002 to 2013: Theory development, empirical evidence, and future research focus. *Educational Management Administration & Leadership, 44*(1), 146–164.

Trilling, B., & Fadel, C. (2009). *21st century skills: Learning for life in our times*. San Francisco: John Wiley & Sons.

Tucker, M. (Ed.). (2011). *Surpassing Shanghai: An agenda for American education built on the world's leading systems*. Boston: Harvard Education Press.

Tyack, D., & Cuban, L. (1995). *Tinkering toward utopia: A century of public school reform*. Cambridge, MA: Harvard University Press.

Tyack, D., & Tobin, W. (1994). The "grammar" of schooling: Why has it been so hard to change? *American Educational Research Journal, 31*(3), 453–479.

United Nations. *Convention on the rights of the child, November 20, 1989*. Retrieved from https://www.ohchr.org/en/professionalinterest/pages/crc.aspx

Vallerand, R. J. (2016). The dualistic model of passion: Theory, research, and implications for the field of education. In W. C. Liu, J. C. K. Wang, & R. M. Ryan (Eds.), *Building autonomous learners: Perspectives from research and practice using self-determination theory* (pp. 31–58). Singapore: Springer.

van Inwagen, P. (2008). How to think about the problem of free will. *The Journal of Ethics, 12*(3), 327–341.

Vansteenkiste, M., Niemiec, C., & Soenens, B. (2010). The development of the five mini-theories of self-determination theory: An historical overview, emerging trends, and future directions. In T. Urdan & S. Karabenick (Eds.), *Advances in motivation and achievement, vol. 16: The decade ahead*. Bingley, UK: Emerald Publishing.

Vella-Brodrick, D. A., Rickard, N. S., & Chin, T-C. (2014). *An evaluation of positive education at Geelong Grammar School: A snapshot of 2013*. Retrieved from https://www.ggs.vic.edu.au/ArticleDocuments/889/Research%20Report-GGS-August2014.pdf.aspx

Waghid, Y. (2014). *Pedagogy out of bounds: Untamed variations of democratic education* (Vol. 61). New York: Springer Science & Business Media.

Wagner, T. (2008). The *global achievement gap: Why even our best schools don't teach the new survival skills our children need—and what we can do about it*. New York: Basic Books.

Wagner, T. (2012). *Creating innovators: The making of young people who will change the world*. New York: Scribner.

Washor, E., & Mojkowski, C. (2014). Student disengagement: It's deeper than you think. *Phi Delta Kappan, 95*(8), 8–10.

Wehmeyer, M. L., Agran, M., & Hughes, C. (1998). *Teaching self-determination to students with disabilities: Basic skills for successful transition*. Baltimore: Paul H. Brookes.

Wehmeyer, M. L., Agran, M., Palmer, S. B., & Mithaug, D. E. (1999). *A teacher's guide to implementing the self-determined learning model of instruction*. Lawrence, KS: Beach Center on Disability.

Wehmeyer, M. L., Little, T., & Sergeant, J. (2009). Self-determination. In S. Lopez & R. Snyder (Eds.), *Handbook of positive psychology* (2nd ed., pp. 357–366). Oxford: Oxford University Press.

Wehmeyer, M. L., & Mithaug, D. (2006). Self-determination, causal agency, and mental retardation. In L. M. Glidden (Ed.), *International Review of Research in Mental Retardation* (Vol. 31) (pp. 31–71). San Diego, CA: Academic Press.

Wehmeyer, M. L. & Shogren, K. A. (2017). Decision-making. In M. L. Wehmeyer, K. A. Shogren, T. D. Little, & S. J. Lopez (Eds.), *Development of self-determination through the life-course* (pp. 261–270). New York: Springer.

Weinstein, N., Przybylski, A. K., & Ryan, R. M. (2012). The index of autonomous functioning: Development of a scale of human autonomy. *Journal of Research in Personality, 46*(4), 397–413. doi: 10.1016/j.jrp.2012.03.007

Weinstein, N., & Ryan, R. M. (2010). When helping helps: Autonomous motivation for prosocial behavior and its influence on well-being for the helper and recipient. *Journal of Personality and Social Psychology, 98*(2), 222–244.

Wilby, P. (2016, June 07). Sugata Mitra—the professor with his head in the cloud. *The Guardian*. Retrieved from https://www.theguardian.com/education/2016/jun/07/sugata-mitra-professor-school-in-cloud

Wilson, K. E., Vyakarnam, S., Volkmann, C., Mariotti, S., & Rabuzzi, D. (2009). Educating the next wave of entrepreneurs: Unlocking entrepreneurial capabilities to meet the global challenges of the 21st century. *World Economic Forum: A Report of the Global Education Initiative.* Retrieved from https://ssrn.com/abstract=1396704

Woolley, K., & Fishbach, A. (2017). Immediate rewards predict adherence to long-term goals. *Personality and Social Psychology Bulletin, 43*(2), 151–162.

World Economic Forum. (2016). *The future of jobs: Employment, skills, and workforce strategy for the fourth industrial revolution.* Retrieved from http://www3.weforum.org/docs/WEF_Future_of_Jobs.pdf

World Economic Forum Global Education Initiative. (2011). *Unlocking entrepreneurial capabilities to meet the global challenged of the 21st century: Final report on the entrepreneurship education work stream.* Retrieved from http://www3.weforum.org/docs/WEF_GEI_UnlockingEntrepreneurialCapabilities_Report_2011.pdf

Wren, D. J. (1999). School culture: Exploring the hidden curriculum. *Adolescence, 34*(135), 593–596.

Zhang, G., & Zhao, Y. (2014). Achievement gap in China. In J. V. Clark (Ed.), *Closing the achievement gap from an international perspective: Transforming STEM for effective education* (pp. 217–228). New York: Springer.

Zhao, Y. (2009a). *Catching up or leading the way: American education in the age of globalization.* Alexandria, VA: ASCD.

Zhao, Y. (2009b). Needed: Global villagers. *Educational Leadership, 67*(1), 60–65.

Zhao, Y. (2012). *World class learners: Educating creative and entrepreneurial students.* Thousand Oaks, CA: Corwin Press.

Zhao, Y. (2014). *Who's afraid of the big bad dragon: Why China has the best (and worst) education system in the world.* San Francisco: Jossey-Bass.

Zhao, Y. (2015a). *Lessons that matter: What should we learn from Asia's school systems?* Retrieved from http:// www.mitchellinstitute.org.au/reports/lessons-that-matter-what-should-we-learn-from -asias-school -systems/

Zhao, Y. (2015b). A world at risk: An imperative for a paradigm shift to cultivate 21st century learners. *Society, 52*(2), 129–135.

Zhao, Y. (2016a). *Counting what counts: Reframing education outcomes.* Bloomington, IN: Solution Tree.

Zhao, Y. (2016b). From deficiency to strength: Shifting the mindset about education inequality. *Journal of Social Issues, 72*(4), 716–735.

Zhao, Y. (2018a). Personalizable education for greatness. *Kappa Delta Pi Record, 54*(3), 109–115.

Zhao, Y. (2018b). *Reach for greatness: Personalizable education for all children.* Thousand Oaks, CA: Corwin Press.

Zhao, Y. (2018c). The rise of the useless: The case for talent diversity. *Journal of Science Education and Technology, 28*(1), 62–68. doi:10.1007/s10956-018-9743-3

Zhao, Y. (2018d). Shifting the education paradigm: Why international borrowing is no longer sufficient for improving education in China. *ECNU Review of Education, 1*(1), 76–106.

Zhao, Y. (2018e). *What works may hurt: Side effects in education.* New York: Teachers College Press.

Zhao, Y., & Gearin, B. (Eds.). (2018). *Imagining the future of global education: Dreams and nightmares.* New York: Routledge.

Zhao, Y., Zhang, G., Lei, J., & Qiu, W. (2015). *Never send a human to do a machine's job: Correcting the top five mistakes in Ed Tech.* Thousand Oaks, CA: Corwin Press.

Index

The letter *f* following a page number denotes a figure.

About the Authors

 Michael Wehmeyer, PhD, is the Ross and Marianna Beach distinguished professor and chairperson, Department of Special Education, at the University of Kansas. His scholarly work has focused on understanding and promoting self-determination and self-determined learning, creating and evaluating autonomy-supportive interventions, and the application of positive psychology to the disability context. He has published extensively in these areas and is an author or editor of more than 40 books and more than 400 scholarly articles and book chapters. Wehmeyer is a member of the Phi Beta Delta Honor Society for International Scholars and an honorary alumni inductee of the Phi Beta Kappa Arts and Sciences Honor Society. He has held numerous leadership and editorial positions in the field and has been recognized for his research and service with awards from numerous associations and organizations, including the American Psychological Association Distinguished Contributions to the Advancement of Disability Issues in Psychology Award. Wehmeyer holds graduate degrees in special education and experimental psychology from the University of Tulsa and the University of Sussex in Brighton, England, respectively, and earned his PhD in Human Development and Communication Sciences from the University of Texas at Dallas, where he received a 2014 Distinguished Alumni Award.

Yong Zhao is foundation distinguished professor in the School of Education at the University of Kansas. Prior to joining the University of Kansas, he served as the presidential chair, director of the Institute for Global and Online Education, and associate dean in the College of Education, University of Oregon, where he was also a professor in the Department of Educational Measurement, Policy, and Leadership. Until December 2010, Zhao was a University

Distinguished Professor at the College of Education, Michigan State University, where he also served as the founding director of the Center for Teaching and Technology and executive director of the Confucius Institute and the US-China Center for Research on Educational Excellence.

Zhao has published more than 100 articles and 30 books, including *What Works May Hurt: Side Effects in Education* (2018), *Reach for Greatness: Personalizable Education for all Children* (2018), *Counting What Counts: Reframing Education Outcomes* (2016), *Never Send a Human to Do a Machine's Job: Correcting Top 5 Ed Tech Mistakes* (2015), *Who's Afraid of the Big Bad Dragon: Why China Has the Best (and Worst) Education System in the World* (2014), *Catching Up or Leading the Way: American Education in the Age of Globalization* (2009), and *World-Class Learners: Educating Creative and Entrepreneurial Students* (2012).

Zhao has received numerous awards, including the Early Career Award from the American Educational Research Association, Outstanding Public Educator from Horace Mann League of USA, and Distinguished Achievement Award in Professional Development from the Association of Education Publishers. He is an elected fellow of the International Academy for Education and is recognized as one of the most influential education scholars.

Related ASCD Resources

At the time of publication, the following resources were available (ASCD stock numbers appear in parentheses):

Print Products

Students at the Center: Personalized Learning with Habits of Mind by Bena Kallick and Allison Zmuda (#117015)

Teaching Students to Drive Their Brains: Metacognitive Strategies, Activities, and Lesson Ideas by Donna Wilson and Marcus Conyers (#117002)

The Motivated Brain: Improving Student Attention, Engagement, and Perseverance by Gayle Gregory and Martha Kaufeldt (#115041)

Learning to Choose, Choosing to Learn by Mike Anderson (#116015)

Learning-Driven Schools: A Practical Guide for Teachers and Principals by Barry Beers (#106002)

Catching Up or Leading the Way: American Education in the Age of Globalization by Yong Zhao (#109076)

ASCD myTeachSource®

Download resources from a professional learning platform with hundreds of research-based best practices and tools for your classroom at http://myteach-source.ascd.org/.

For more information, send an e-mail to member@ascd.org; call 1-800-933-2723 or 703-578-9600; send a fax to 703-575-5400; or write to Information Services, ASCD, 1703 N. Beauregard St., Alexandria, VA 22311-1714 USA.

WHOLE CHILD
TENETS

1 **HEALTHY**
Each student enters school healthy and learns about and practices a healthy lifestyle.

2 **SAFE**
Each student learns in an environment that is physically and emotionally safe for students and adults.

3 **ENGAGED**
Each student is actively engaged in learning and is connected to the school and broader community.

4 **SUPPORTED**
Each student has access to personalized learning and is supported by qualified, caring adults.

5 **CHALLENGED**
Each student is challenged academically and prepared for success in college or further study and for employment and participation in a global environment.

THE WHOLE CHILD

The ASCD Whole Child approach is an effort to transition from a focus on narrowly defined academic achievement to one that promotes the long-term development and success of all children. Through this approach, ASCD supports educators, families, community members, and policymakers as they move from a vision about educating the whole child to sustainable, collaborative actions.

Teaching Students to Become Self-Determined Learners relates to the **healthy**, **safe**, and **engaged** tenets.

For more about the ASCD Whole Child approach, visit **www. ascd.org/wholechild.**